D0101024

Good Morning, Corfu

A Year on a Greek Island

MADDIE GRIGG

*'Other countries may offer you discoveries in manners or lore or landscape.
Greece offers you something harder: the discovery of yourself.'*

Laurence Durrell

To the Alexakis Family
for showing us the meaning of
philoxenia

Prologue

I am swimming in a sheltered cove on Corfu's west coast, the warm water funnelling through my fingertips. It is so clear, it's like looking through a pane of glass. The sun ripples across the surface, sending shadows diving down to dance on the sandy bottom. A fish brushes my leg, ever so gently.

Back on the shore, with its cluster of sunbeds and blue umbrellas, the birds and cicadas chirrup among the clean, aromatic pines, as if singing was the most natural thing in the world, which indeed it is. This is a lovely, peaceful spot.

From the water, I gaze out to sea towards a distinctive outcrop of rock. Mythology (and tourist operators) claim it's the petrified ship of the ancient hero, Odysseus. It is said that the ship was turned to stone by Poseidon, the god of the ocean, because he was angry at the natives for helping Odysseus reach his homeland on Ithaca. In the ten years it took the homesick Odysseus to get from Troy to his beloved island south of Corfu, Poseidon was a terrifying force. The god sent cataclysmic storms and monsters to punish Odysseus for blinding his son, Polyphemus the Cyclops.

There are several stony contenders for Odysseus' ship around the island of Corfu, which the Greeks know as Kerkyra and, in The Odyssey, Homer calls Scheria. These rocks can't all be the same vessel. But it could quite as easily have been here in this spot, in my secluded cove, as anywhere else. In the end, none of it really matters, because who knows if Odysseus and his ship ever existed.

Mythology is a state of mind. In Greece, and on the island of Corfu, it's all around you. You can see it, feel it, breathe it, hear it, smell it and taste it. It's in the wind rustling through the leaves of the oak trees… in the heady scent of jasmine and orange blossom…and the mouth-watering smell of roast lamb on a spit; it's in the ethereal sight of fireflies on a warm spring night, and in the hospitality of strangers. Mythology and the endearing

7

nature of the Greek spirit are as much a part of this island as the olive trees, the cypresses, the vivid blue sky and the turquoise sea gently caressing the white pebbles and sand.

Here in Corfu, it's easy to imagine being in an ancient land.

And as I float on my back, in my head I am Homer's princess, Nausika, having a quiet soak after playing ball with my maids, with the shipwrecked Odysseus watching from the shallows.

I am in this trance-like state when the other side of this beautiful island kicks in. I can hear the sound of English voices singing in the distance, accompanied by a booming soundtrack: 'Feeling hot, hot, hot…' I open my eyes, stand up and look out to the horizon. My carefully constructed vision of ancient Greece is crudely pierced, not by a sharpened staff of green olive wood, the mast of some black ship with twenty oars, but by a tripper boat bobbing up and down next to the very rock that a few seconds ago was Odysseus's petrified vessel. I can just about make out a dozen figures standing on the top of the rock, some of them diving in. There is whooping, hollering, splashing and raucous wailing.

My peace has been momentarily shattered.

But I don't mind. It's all part and parcel of the enigma of this place. Corfu has something for everyone. It just depends on what you want.

I think about what drew me here, after a lifetime of living in England's south west and leading a life quite ordinary. I see lush green fields and bluebell woods, family and friends and a village of quaint cottages with roses around the doors. Up on high somewhere, Mount Olympus maybe, the goddess wiggles her fingers in the waters of the divining bowl to reveal a similar village on Corfu, with pink, terracotta and cream-coloured houses, and bougainvillea, grapevines and orange blossom clamouring for attention. There are Elysian Fields of asphodel, olive groves and waves a-plenty from smiley-faced people on scooters, in trucks and on foot. And then, in this period of reflection, I see my husband, my own Odysseus, standing on a rocky ledge preparing to dive into the shimmering water. Under the surface, he swims like a fish towards me and emerges, the sunlight glinting on his fleshy shoulders. He has a grin the size of Ithaca across his face.

'Kalimera,' he says. 'We are okay?'

And right at this moment, yes, I am.

Part I

Autumn

'Every man has his folly, but the greatest folly of all, in my view, is not to have one.'

Nikos Kazantzakis, *Zorba the Greek*

September

I was a solitary, middle-aged woman in a bright orange dress, sitting alone in the darkness, staring at the flames of the fire in the great hall at Forde Abbey, a historic mansion on the borders of Dorset, Somerset and Devon. From my perch on a stool in the vast room, with its oak-panelled ceiling and huge, gilt-framed oil paintings, I could hear the noise travelling up through the orangery, as the wedding guests whooped it up in the undercroft, where the reception went on into the night. I prodded the fire with a poker. I was deep in thought.

We were at the wedding of a friend's daughter and I'd just had an argument with my husband, who was tripping the light fantastic with the others while I sat on my own in a swirl of self-pity. It was all a bit of a worry because, in two days' time, we were driving from southern England to Greece to spend twelve months on Corfu, for our very own grown-up gap year. We were letting out our house in our village in Dorset (although we hadn't yet found a tenant) and renting a place on the island. We wanted to see what our favourite holiday destination was like all year round.

It was one of those 'opportunity of a lifetime' decisions.

But this evening, as Eric Clapton sang 'Wonderful Tonight' in the distance, I was gazing into a dwindling fire and having second thoughts. The floaty shift dress I swore had looked great on me when I'd tried it on in the changing room of the department store in Dorchester made me feel like Tango Woman: fat, round and orangey. My husband had spent half the afternoon drinking too much and then absent-mindedly stroking the neck of a random woman sitting next to him. He had insisted on wearing a pocket watch from one of his previous wives and then decided to do the gallant thing and waltz the night away with the most beautiful woman at the wedding. Admittedly she was the bride's step-grandmother and eighty-six years old but, honestly, you'd have thought he'd have a bit of time for me, knowing how uncertain I was about our year away.

I peered into the fire, hoping for divine inspiration from Hestia, the Greek goddess of the hearth. Every now and then I leaned forward with the poker to prod a smouldering log, which I pretended was my husband. Over and over in my head, I could hear someone who sounded very like me saying, '*Do I really want to go to Greece for a year and, if the answer is yes, do I really want to go with him?*'

We enjoyed a see-saw relationship at the best of times, with the balance of power constantly shifting. He's a leader, I'm an ideas person and I won't always follow his lead. This year away had to be a joint decision, something for both of us, and it *was*. But right at that moment, I wasn't sure I actually wanted to spend every hour of the day in a foreign country with the man I'd married. He's chalk, I'm cheese. He's Tory, I'm Labour. He's gregarious, I'm an observer. We're opposites and we shouldn't have attracted. But we had. And in many ways, our differences made us stronger. But to be together twenty-four hours a day?

It was all right for him. He was sixty-one and ready for early retirement. But I was ten years younger and fiercely independent. I have always worked, even with two children in tow, and, from the age of eighteen, have had my own money. Was I too young to give that all up for a romantic whim?

The day of the wedding was one of the few, rain-free days we'd had for months. Rather like the Durrells who, in the 1930s, decided to up sticks for Corfu after looking out onto a rainy Bournemouth seafront, we were ready for some sunshine. We'd had the worst summer in England since records began. There'd been howling winds, storms and floods and our part of the county had hit the headlines for all the wrong reasons. Down on the coast, a sodden cliff had crashed down on the beach, wiping out a young woman who'd had the whole of her life ahead of her. It was a terrible tragedy. Inland, just a few miles away from us, there was a landslip at Beaminster Tunnel, which collapsed on a couple returning from an evening meal. They didn't get out alive. It was one of the saddest local news stories I had read in years. For us, those terrible accidents brought into stark relief the importance of seizing the day. You just never knew when your number was up.

So when a nurse told my husband during his annual health check-up that he had a three in ten chance of having a heart attack, it seemed as good a time as any to pack up and bugger off from real life for a year. As regular visitors to the Greek island of Corfu, which sits in the Ionian Sea just off the mainland coast, we had always wondered what it would be like in autumn and winter. If I'd been on that television programme, *A Place in the Sun,* I would have been telling the presenter: 'If we don't do it now, Jasmine, we never will.' And if we never did it, we might regret it for the rest of our lives.

That's what I kept telling myself. Now I was not so sure.

'How will you cope?' my best friend asked me on the morning of the wedding. I was holding onto her elbow as I teetered in high heels up the lane to the church. The bridal party strolled into view, making its way into the village square through a street lined with home-made bunting and colourful hanging baskets. The bride's father, resplendent in a tartan kilt, ambled up the road, arm-in-arm with his beautiful daughter, dark-haired, eager-eyed, smiling and radiant. The bride's stepmother, a vision in navy blue, scooped up the long, white bridal train as the party approached the shallow steps to the church. A chorus of villagers, gathered around the newly-painted telephone box, smiled and cooed in unison. Had it not been for the odd car driving by and, of course, the telephone box, we could have been in the pages of a Thomas Hardy novel.

It was so very *English.* I was going to miss this place.

But the answer to my friend's question came easily. I'd been practising it for a while.

'Oh, I'll be fine, it'll be the experience of a lifetime,' I said, thinking of sun, sea, the chance to focus on writing fiction and all good things Greek. Who wouldn't jack in the day job given the opportunity? I told my friend a change was as good as a rest and recited every other platitude that came to hand.

'But what about the language barrier?' she said. We didn't speak very good Greek. 'And won't you be homesick? Won't you miss the grandchildren? Won't you miss having your own money?'

To be honest, I hadn't really given it much thought. If I had, we might never have been going. Why think about the negatives when the positives far outweighed them? We'd be living the dream, if only for a year, and what was difficult about that? And when people asked me '*why?*' my answer was always '*why not?*' But now, at the eleventh hour, my feet were getting just a little bit cold. Twelve months with a newly-retired husband with time on his hands and me giving up an enjoyable and well-paid job with colleagues I liked. What on earth was I thinking? Sure, it would give me time to write, but would what I wrote be any good?

As the day of our departure grew ever closer I could relate to the phrase '*Be careful what you wish for*'. There was nowhere to hide.

Sitting in the village church for the wedding service, the doubts went around and around in my head, just as the couple exchanged their vows. They were standing in front of a stone altar bearing the chiselled sentence '*This Do In Remembrance of Me*'. The word order had always seemed out of kilter to me. It was more like an instruction from Yoda, the Jedi Master from *Star Wars,* than Jesus.

I stared up at the vaulted ceiling, marvelling at the beautiful simplicity of this ancient building. I'm a sucker for ecclesiastic architecture but there was no chance of God tuning into my thoughts because we were not on speaking terms. I'm an atheist, albeit with agnostic tendencies veering towards paganism. In my world, the ancient Greek pantheon, Native American spirits, the Norse gods, Buddha, fairies, God and Allah all have as good a claim as any to be our guiding forces. I don't believe in anything much, although I like the whimsical idea of all these gods and magic creatures living side by side, and being anything anyone wants them to be. It's not that I'm disrespectful of people's beliefs, rituals and traditions, having been brought up in a strong Church of England household. Whatever floats your boat is all right by me, as long as it doesn't hurt anyone. I believe in the power of nature and the essential goodness of humanity. The human race has the ability to overcome anything and everything but very rarely does, preferring instead to get caught up in hatred, conflict and materialism. As the soul singer Timmy Thomas said in 1973, why can't we live together?

16

The service over, we spilled out into the square and climbed aboard one of three large buses to the reception. We drove down through the village, up the hill and out into the lush Dorset countryside. As a farmer's daughter, born and bred just thirteen miles away, I realised I was attached to this landscape more than I knew. I had never really been very far away from home; a few years in Plymouth in the early 1980s training as a journalist after leaving school and then to Bridport. And I had been in Dorset ever since.

With my husband at my side chatting to other passengers about our forthcoming Greek adventure, I saw the county's highest point, the tree-clad Lewesdon Hill, and then the flat top of Pilsdon Pen (which, in my mind and that of other locals, will always be the taller of the two, despite what Ordnance Survey says). The wedding guests from London craned their necks to the left and gasped at the lovely view out across the Marshwood Vale. From here we could see Colmers Hill, with its handful of fir trees waving in the distance, towards the cliffs of Eype Down, Thorncombe Beacon and Golden Cap, the highest cliff on the south coast, and then the shimmering sea beyond. It's a gorgeous spot, this part of Dorset, this England. And I love it very much.

I was in this frame of mind when we arrived, through the winding lanes, at Forde Abbey. It's an ancient and stately building, mellow stone anchored in a sea of green lawn, with age-old trees and fields in the background. Elegant ladies in floaty pastel dresses with matching fascinators in their hair mingled with the men in suits on the terrace. I wandered away from the throng and up the grass bank to capture the scene with my long-lens camera. Guests were laughing, there was a clutch of a shoulder here and a kiss on the cheek there. There were wedding hats and morning suits, flowing and flowery skirts and a splash of tartan.

I adjusted the lens and focused on my husband as he came into view. He was laughing, joking and the centre of attention. I glanced down at my painted toes in sandals that really didn't go with my hideous Tango Woman dress and remembered how we had found our house on Corfu just a few months earlier.

17

The key was in the lock but the front door refused to open.

'I don't know what's happened,' the agent said, trying to push the door with her shoulder. 'It was all right when I came up yesterday.'

We were standing on the side of the road in a hillside village in north west Corfu. It was a warm day in June and the cicadas were chirruping as loudly as ever. We were about to view a third rental property and the search wasn't going too well. While the agent struggled with the key and became more and more flustered, my husband tried to give her a helping hand. I sloped off and opened a side gate into the garden, with its view of olive trees and cypresses on a distant hillside, tumbling down to an invisible sea. I took a deep breath and inhaled the smell of pine, herbs and hot, dusty roads.

'What a lovely place,' I thought to myself. 'I could write here.'

Five minutes later and still in a trance, I was back at the front door. They were no closer to getting inside. A man working on the neighbouring house ambled over and tried to prise open the lock with a screwdriver but without success. He shouted to his workmate, a young Albanian, who walked across and attempted to break in by forcing the handle with brute strength. But the door wouldn't yield.

'There have been a few problems with this place,' the agent finally said, as we huddled around the door getting nowhere. 'The owner wanted me to tell you she's quite happy to put it back into the state it was in before the last tenant moved in.'

Alarm bells rang in my head. *A few problems? The state it was in before the last tenant moved in?* I turned away from the door and walked back into the garden to reacquaint myself with the view and the good feeling I'd first had about this place. I tripped over a long dog lead, narrowly missed a pile of mess belonging to the same animal in the coarse grass; and I became aware of a broken manhole cover on the lawn. And then the smell of herbs that had earlier wafted around so obligingly was replaced by the sickly sweet aroma of dog shit and Greek drains. How quickly a place can change.

The workman continued to struggle with the lock and screwdriver.

'The woman who live here, she move out yesterday,' he said. 'Maybe she not want you to get in.'

Suddenly, his young friend declared that he had the answer. With the agility of a gecko, he shot up a drainpipe to an upstairs balcony, felt around the window, pulled up the mosquito screen and, *hey presto*, he was in.

From the outside, we could hear him coming towards us down the stairs to the front door. It sounded as if he was running. From the inside, he opened the door with ease. But instead of ushering us in, the young man rushed out, slamming the door behind him and slapping his arms and legs.

I shuddered.

Fleas.

And then the agent, my husband and the workman and I all began to itch frantically, a psychosomatic reaction to the teeming infestation inside.

'We can get it fumigated for you,' the agent said, rubbing the inside of her elbow.

We smiled as we scratched; but she knew she was out on a limb. Our list of possible houses was diminishing and we were running out of time. We had given ourselves three days to find the perfect house to rent for a year. But it wasn't meant to be. It did not exist.

The despondency hung in our hire car like a Dorset mist as we drove back to Corfu Town, the lovely capital whose old parts are the prettiest in Greece.

My husband's dream of letting our house in the UK and renting somewhere on Corfu for twelve months was ridiculous, especially with the Greek economy at its very worst and austerity measures beginning to bite, even in the islands. But it had seemed the answer to our prayers a few months earlier when we'd looked out of our English window onto a never-ending view of rain. And I had gone along with it, quite happily. Twelve months in the sun was the perfect antidote to the English summer and it would be good for his health, too. But both of us were agreed that it all hinged on finding the *right* house. We knew we'd know it, if and when we found it. And if we found it, we'd do it. We'd been waiting for some sort of sign, not necessarily a dramatic break in the clouds and a big booming voice from

19

above saying 'this is the one', but a sign nonetheless. This was Greece after all, the land of ancient magic. But, at this rate, it wasn't going to happen.

Our hire car dragged its way up the mountainside, as downhearted as its occupants. Suddenly, behind us, there was a screech of tyres and the agent's car came past. Like some sort of crazed hen, she flapped her arm out of the window in a signal which stated very clearly that she wanted us to stop.

'I've had an idea!' she shouted as we drew up alongside. 'I've got to go to another house to take some photos. It's in a village I always think of as one of my top three on the island. Would you like to come and have a look?'

We sighed. We'd never heard of the village she was talking about. She sounded too desperate. It was bound to be another wild goose chase. What would be in this one? Goats, maybe? Or perhaps wild geese? But we had nothing to lose, so we followed her car as she drove around a double hairpin bend.

'Remember this?' I said to my husband, as we drove down from Trompeta to see the lush scenery lying out before us. 'It's not far from where Emma Tennant's family had that lovely home on the beach.'

We had found the Glenconnner villa, Rovinia, several years earlier after I had finished reading Tennant's book, *A House in Corfu*, in which she describes what happened after her parents fell in love with the spot near Paleokastritsa when they saw it from the deck of a cruise ship. They returned, bought the plot of land, built a house and lived there for forty years.

We followed the agent down the hill and turned off the main road, through winding olive groves and into a sleepy village square, not unlike our own in Dorset. An elderly woman sitting outside a taverna gave us that cheery wave only the Greeks seem to give, showing the back of her hand and waggling her fingers as if she was beckoning. We drove on and parked on the outskirts, just above a primary school, where the shrieks of Greek children at play filled the air with vitality and joy. We got out of the car and admired the view across to the valley floor and then up to mountains. And then we followed the agent from the car park down a short drive dominated by a very tall palm tree.

'Welcome to the Villa Oleander,' she said, opening the metal gate of a modern house which, at first sight, seemed to have very little character. With the key in the lock, we held our breath, not wanting a repetition of the last place but not daring to hope for anything better.

We gasped as we were hit by the light and airy interior, floating before us above a floor of terracotta bricks. There was a cosy, striped sofa and rows of shelves full of novels and reference books next to a large open fireplace with classic, Adams-like proportions. The house's thick walls opened up into a series of sweeping arches leading off from a central hall to living and dining rooms, a utility room and a kitchen. There were three bedrooms upstairs, one of which was en-suite, a family bathroom and three toilets; an upstairs balcony looking out on that view I'd seen from the car park and an outside eating area accessed through French windows and nestling under a vine. There was even what looked like a swimming pool outside. The separate parts shouldn't have worked together as a whole but they did. Something about the place felt very right.

'Do you like it?' the agent asked.

'Like it? It's fantastic,' I said and then instantly wished I hadn't, because I knew we wouldn't be able to afford it.

'I thought you would,' the agent said. 'It belongs to a writer.'

A sign.

The house was like a favourite coat rediscovered after years of being left on the peg. It was familiar, it fitted, it was cosy and it felt like home. It's true the house needed a good clean; but it would scrub up. The garden, though, was like a jungle. Great oleander trees as tall as giraffes and a palm as big as an elephant concealed a stagnant swimming pool with hidden horrors underneath its cover. It would take a whole tribe of gardeners to do something with that. The garden was dark and it was crying out to be reacquainted with the glorious Greek light.

'I want this house,' I said, squeezing my husband's arm as we crunched across the fallen palm leaves that littered the edge of the pool. 'There's something about it.'

As we left and the front door closed behind us, I looked at the hands on my watch. They were in exactly the same position as they had been when we'd gone in.

21

Another sign.

Later, in Corfu Town, over a coffee on the Liston, that lovely, majestic row of arcaded buildings built by the French and modelled on the Rue de Rivoli in Paris, the pair of us had an earnest discussion.

'It's lovely,' my husband said, keeping an eye on the game of cricket underway on the grassy area which is part of the Spianada overlooking the sea. 'But I think it's going to be a bit over our budget. And, anyway, I'm not sure you really want to do this year away, do you?'

I hadn't been sure myself until I'd visited the house. But the Villa Oleander had other ideas. I was so fickle. It had clearly cast a spell on me. Looking out beyond the cricket pitch to the old fort, I thought what a lovely place this would be to call home.

I squirmed on my seat.

The words were out of my mouth before I could stop them. 'Well, I *can* see us living there, can't you?' I said.

I had sealed my own fate. From that point onwards, I was in.

It was the right house, we both knew that. Apart from the 'signs', it was homely, away from the tourist crowds and on the edge of what appeared to be a pretty and thriving village. It had a really good feel to it. But could we afford it?

My attention was drawn to a pigeon doing a circular dance on the pavement around a female bird. All along the Liston, the pigeons were courting each other, only for their ritual to be suddenly interrupted by a large black man touting knocked-off DVDs to anyone foolish enough to give him eye contact. We knew about these DVDs. My husband had once been stupid enough to buy three for ten euros when we were on holiday here a few years before. I had warned him not to. I knew that pirated movies funded all sorts of horrible things, even if buying them meant money for the African man to send home to his family. But it was no good. The moral dilemma escaped my husband. Back in the UK, we sat down to watch *Cowboys and Aliens* (not one of Daniel Craig's finest moments) only to find that every now and then, the silhouette of a woman with a big bun hairstyle would get up from the audience and go down through the auditorium, probably to the toilet, before coming back again five minutes later.

The pigeons were obviously wise to the fact that, despite his wide grin, the looky-looky man was indeed bad news. In unison, they flew away from him, up to the safety of the first floor windows of the Liston, coming down again only when the danger had passed.

On the cricket pitch, the batsman had just been caught out when my husband's phone rang.

'Yes,' he said, speaking into it. And then he paused. 'I think we can manage that.'

He said a few more things, the pigeons flew off a couple more times and another batsman took over, and then my husband put the phone down on the table.

'Well …?' I said, as a pigeon attempted to pin down the female it had its eye on.

'It's ours.'

'Really?'

The female had no escape.

'Yes. We've done a deal. A reduced rent in exchange for doing a few jobs around the house. The agent just needs a banker's reference, a personal reference and a deposit.'

There was a fleeting look of terror on the female pigeon's face.

'It'll give me something to do,' my husband said. 'And it'll give you the chance to write.'

The female pigeon put her head to one side and mirrored the male's movements.

A year in Corfu, our own fantasy island.

Later that day, we found ourselves at the tax office, a grubby five-storey building faced in light grey marble, with air conditioning units outside every window. Teenage boys used the front courtyard as a skateboard ramp and a melange of mopeds and scooters were parked against a low wall. Inside, the staff were dressed casually, in polo shirts, jeans and trainers. A ticket machine spewed out a piece of paper with a number on it and we waited in turn, as if we were standing at the deli counter at Morrisons for two Scotch eggs and four slices of ham. A young man with the chiselled face of an ancient Greek shuffled large bundles of paper very loudly, making his presence felt in a hubbub of foreign voices. And then, after ten minutes, we were at the front of the queue. A few signatures, lots of stamping and we were done. We now had our own tax numbers which meant we were legally entitled to rent a house on the island. Next stop was the Bank of Cyprus to open up a Greek account.

We emerged under darkening skies, absorbing the hustle and bustle around us, breathing it all in, breathing in the air of our island. With our own tax numbers we were more than just holidaymakers, we were part of this island. And just at the point that this dawned on us, it began to rain. And rain and rain and rain. As I was wearing an Accessorize hat made from woven paper which was clearly labelled 'Do not get wet', we headed for the nearest doorway.

'It's the first rain for weeks,' an Englishman said to us as he sheltered outside the same shop. 'And I'm so excited.'

Zeus be praised, I thought. Another sign. The gods were looking kindly on us.

So I handed in my notice, my husband wound down and took early retirement and we decided to head for Corfu in October 2012, driving in convoy in my ancient VW Beetle and my husband's Land Rover with everything we would need for our year away. Our friends were bereft and there was a mixed reaction from family, with the early twenty-somethings saying, 'Yes, you go for it;' and then older ones who ought to know better laying on the guilt trip by bawling their eyes out and saying how much they would miss us and did we really have to go. My elderly parents were non-committal and our siblings very excited, even when one of them realised they'd have to take care of our cats for a year.

It was strange to be relocating to a country undergoing its biggest crisis in years. News reports said Greece was on its knees. Its economy was in tatters, there were protests on the streets of Athens and people were homeless, angry and hungry. Meanwhile, the very rich, as is always the case, were getting away with it. The widely-held view of the ordinary man or woman in the street was that the politicians were corrupt and the people at the bottom of the pile would never prosper. Before we left, our friends in England were fearful for our future.

'You could be killed,' they said. 'It looks terrible on the television news.'

'We'll be all right,' we said. 'Greece has been through worse times.'

And we also knew that, on a tourist island, things were never going to be quite as bad as in the big cities. But only time would tell.

'Well,' one colleague said on my last day at work. 'I suppose it makes some kind of sense, leaving one bankrupt country for another.'

'It would make a great book,' said another colleague as I opened up my leaving card and wept at all the kind words contained inside. 'You can write about it and at the end you'll find a man. They always find a man at the end.'

'But I'm married,' I said. 'I'm taking my husband with me.'

'Oh, well, darling, that's a shame. Still, maybe you'll find each other.'

Her words rang in my ears as I sat by the hearth in the darkness of the Great Hall at Forde Abbey, prodding the fire rather too aggressively with the poker while my husband was whooping it up with everyone else. It was the best I could hope for.

October

The countdown began as we packed, threw out anything superfluous, took furniture and surplus clothes to a store and sorted through the house that had been our home for the past eleven years.

I faxed the banker's reference to the letting agent in Corfu, along with a short but personal recommendation from the Earl of Sandwich, who had been our landlord when we lived on the lovely estate of Mapperton some years ago. His two-line comment on headed paper stated:

> 'I have known this couple for many years. They are hard-working, reliable and kind.'

It was the perfect reference.

In our suitcases we stashed away gifts from family and friends, which included Jacobs Cream Crackers, Marmite, Manuka honey hand cream and four pairs of silky and lacy knickers (what was my friend thinking?). There were cards from work colleagues and a card from friends which read: 'If anyone's going to fix the Greek economy it's you and Mr Grigg.' And then a handmade card with a child's drawing of a boat on the front and a sad face in the corner. I opened it and read the words aloud:

> 'Goodbye Granny.
> Hope you have a good trip.
> We're going to miss you.'

I found a quiet place upstairs which had not yet been taken over by storage boxes and looked out of the window over our village square, with its shop, pub, water pump, telephone box and steps to the church and children's playground. A mother pushed a little girl on the swing while a second child, with golden hair, climbed up the play fort and came roaring down the slide. She reminded me very much of my seven-year-old granddaughter. A tear rolled down my cheek and then I sobbed, little whimpers at first and then deep, wracking cries. Anyone watching would have thought I was being sent into exile. Living the dream was not meant to feel like this.

A day after the wedding and there were still some things to be done before driving to Corfu. If this story was a film, we'd be flicking through a montage featuring images including a close-up of six, solid burnt pitta breads, like pottery ellipses made from lava, found in the Aga as we cleaned through the house. There'd be a rat running across the garden and a mad scramble to find the poison. We'd be stepping over the plumber and all his tools as he installed a new boiler on our last day in England. The Land Rover had to be serviced, as did the Beetle, a 1969 convertible, in readiness for the epic voyage that lay ahead. There were cardboard boxes stacked up everywhere as we drove backwards and forwards to the storage unit. There was a mystery voice text left on our landline which said, *'Oh buggery bollocks'*. And then there was a party for family and friends in the village hall where an old woman declared in rather a loud voice over an iPod playlist of Greek music: 'I fancy you've put on a little bit of weight, Maddie.'

On the night before we were due to leave, I hosted the village book club, a sombre affair amid all the packing cases and in candlelight because of a power cut. The chilli was too mild, the rice too stodgy, and the whole lot flipped onto the tablecloth via an overladen ladle, taking two candles with it and spraying the book club members with hot wax. The book I'd chosen was torn apart by my friends and by the end of the evening I was more than ready to leave the country.

A day-and-a-half later than planned, it was time to head for Folkestone. After the mad rush to get to this stage, it should have been calm, a blessed relief after all the chaos from the days before. But there was a heated argument over 'Why are we taking all this bloody stuff?' when my husband saw my suitcase full of shoes. I countered his comment with 'Do we really need the spice cupboard and all this chutney?' when I realised what this obsessive foodie was packing into his car. His retort of 'Why you have to take those cushions is beyond me' was met with 'Because my mother embroidered them for my fortieth birthday and having them in Greece will make it feel like home.'

We hadn't even left and we already hated each other.

We intended to set off just after lunch but finally left at five o'clock in the afternoon, saying goodbye to the village in our two-vehicle convoy. We got ten miles down the road to fill up with petrol and my husband lost his car keys between the pump and the till. After fifteen minutes, we gave up looking for them, left an address with the attendant and used the spare set. In the wind, rain and darkness, the Beetle roof leaked and, behind the steering wheel on the motorway, I could hardly see the Land Rover tail lights in front because my windscreen wipers were going so slowly and in different directions. I saw it as a metaphor for our lives.

We were so delayed in reaching our bed and breakfast near the Channel Tunnel that we stopped off at a service station to stave off our hunger with two Big Macs. We finally arrived at the pub we'd booked into near Ashford at a quarter to ten, each knocked back two pints of Strongbow and then got into an argument, because my husband was glued to football on the big screen whereas he should have been sharing our last moments in England with his wife.

In the morning, the alarm went off at six to give him time to fire up the laptop and pay household bills, write letters and telephone the utility companies to let them know we were leaving the country. His call to BT about cancelling the Broadband was cut off mid-sentence, causing him to issue a long series of expletives and then yell at me for taking the key back to reception rather than leaving it in the door. Before we even entered the Channel Tunnel, he lost two pens, his glasses case and a GB sticker bought five minutes earlier in the AA shop.

It was not a good start. So much for lowering his blood pressure.

After just thirty-five minutes in the tunnel, we were in France. But we discovered the Belgian friend with whom we were meant to be spending our first night was in hospital at his mother's bedside and he could be there for some time. So we

28

changed the route and headed for the Champagne region of France. The next day, the Beetle ground to a halt on an industrial estate on the outskirts of a grey town called Poligny in the Jura region.

'Whose stupid bloody idea was this trip anyway?' I snarled at my husband, as we shuffled our bags across the windswept car park of the Hotel Charmless. The place would not have been out of place on an Alfred Hitchcock film set. It proved to be a sleepless night. In the morning, we could see the hotel was cosied up to a three-lane highway and a busy railway line.

'Well, you wanted to bring the bloody Beetle,' he said. 'You thought it would be fun riding around in it in Corfu during the summer.'

He was right. I was a poseur and this was all my fault.

I argued on the phone with my insurance company who told me that the car was not covered for European breakdown even though they had previously confirmed in writing that it was. It took them four hours and sixteen phone calls to admit they were wrong. And then we were stuck in a small French town for seven days while the garage waited for a new dynamo. Checking out of the Bates Motel, we moved into a gite for a week and got to know the town's best restaurants (all two of them) very well.

And we realised that in all this adversity, we'd stopped bickering.

Each day we called into the garage to find out if the part had arrived, before exploring a damp and foggy Jura. I pitched writing ideas to the *Guardian*, *Telegraph*, *Mslexia* and *Saga Magazine* about our year away, with none of them resulting in anything. The first two didn't bother to reply.

I wanted to go home.

That night, my husband dreamed he was visiting New Zealand for cancer treatment. I dreamed he and I were going to London but as the taxi arrived to take us there, I discovered women's clothes in my wardrobe which weren't mine, which he told me belonged to his 'business partner'. He said he took her to meet clients because she was impressive. It did not take a genius to work out that travel, disappointment and fear of the unknown were uppermost in our minds, even when we were asleep.

On the seventh day, we called into the garage. Not only had the dynamo arrived, it had been fitted. Back on the road again, we set off, my husband leading the way, towards Geneva and then up to the Mont Blanc Tunnel. The Beetle was raring to go and my knuckles were white on the steering wheel as the old girl climbed higher and higher towards the famous tunnel, up the roller-coaster road held up by what seemed like two-mile beanpoles. The toll was a small fortune for such a narrow tunnel but you don't know that until you get there, so there was no turning back.

I followed the Land Rover and drove the Beetle through the tunnel, sitting bolt upright because I was terrified the car was going to break down again. There was no hard shoulder and I really didn't want to block single-handedly the main route across the Alps. But the car held fast until the next morning in Italy when it just wouldn't start. The hotel receptionist called his friend, a young mechanic with filthy teeth who arrived on a scooter an hour or so later and told us in broken English that there was something wrong with the points. He stuck his head in the engine, began working on it and then clocked off for a two-hour lunch break before returning and re-setting the points at forty instead of sixteen. This meant nothing to me until I drove the car. It coughed and spluttered over the next two days, outraged by one of the worst drives of its life, which included being stopped by the police because neither the Beetle nor the Land Rover had their headlights on, which is a requirement when travelling on main roads in Italy.

As the car and I shuddered on to the ferry at Ancona, the relief was palpable. It's as if the car and I could suddenly breathe out for the first time in forty-eight hours.

Now, sleeping with a rug over me in an aircraft seat in a darkened section of the boat where the door slammed as if it was being punched by a giant every time someone went in or out, I dreamed I'd adopted a little girl who had been following me around like a cat. She then turned into a goldfish which I carried in a plastic bag full of water as if I'd won a prize at the funfair. I was walking in my dreams with this girl/cat/fish when, at five in the morning, my husband gave me a nudge.

'Come out on deck and have a look,' he said. 'You won't regret it.'

So I sighed deeply (this terrible journey had been all his fault, after all), climbed out of my seat, banging my knee in the process, and went out through the punchy giant's door. In the fresh air, I stood at the stern with my husband, the only two passengers awake, as daylight broke in true Homeric 'rosy fingered dawn' style over the outline of an island, which waited patiently in the ocean as if to say *what took you so long?* And as we looked out across to Corfu, a crew member raised the Greek flag in a brightening sky full of promise.

There was a wonderful warm, fresh feeling to the air as, car roof down, I clattered off the ferry following the Land Rover and headed away from Corfu Town. After tearing along the main road for a short while, we pulled in to a lorry park at the side of the road to take in our surroundings. We'd made it, and relatively unscathed. Across the water we could see the island curling away from us, dominated by a long, mountainous ridge with a peak at each end, the tallest being Mount Pantokrator, Corfu's highest point. We turned on our heels and gazed out across the Corfu Channel, where the Greek mainland looks very bleak as it nestles up to Albania and the mountains.

And all the homesickness that had travelled alongside me on our incredible journey across Europe evaporated like the fog in our Dorset village. It was going to be fine, really fine. An experience of a lifetime.

We headed north and peeled off the main road just past Skripero, a village with a single traffic light, down through the olive groves where we braked hard to avoid a hundred gobbling turkeys wandering through the trees. They sauntered across the road in front of us, unaware of the fate awaiting them at Christmas in a few months' time. We set off again, just as a small dog charged up through the undergrowth and attempted to attach itself by its teeth to the Beetle's passenger door handle. As we built up speed, the dog gave up and sloped off back through the olive groves. We turned the corner, stopping again as a strong-featured, dark-haired woman herded a line of goats into a clearing. And then we headed up the hill, went around a bend to arrive in the *plateia*, the village square, where we were greeted by a cheering, beckoning wave from the same elderly woman we had seen outside the taverna back in the summer. But we pressed on. It was time to be reacquainted with our new home.

Upon signing the rental agreement, we had discovered that the Villa Oleander belonged to the Tennant family. And just before we arrived in Corfu, two things happened that helped to convince me that our gap year was meant to be. I picked up one of Emma Tennant's novels, *Queen of Stones*, and began to read it. Not only was it set in the part of Dorset I knew so well – the first two villages mentioned being ones I had lived in – but the novel also referred to a report from a fictional local newspaper. It was dated from the same year I had actually joined the real local newspaper, the *Bridport and Lyme Regis News*, as a young reporter back in the 1980s. It didn't matter that this was the novel my book club had torn to shreds. Perhaps I should have taken that as a sign, but I didn't. I was too busy looking for good omens to convince me that the year away was the right thing to do.

And then a strange conversation with my mother clinched it.

'Does it really belong to the Tennants?' she said, as I showed her photographs of the Villa Oleander.

'Yes,' I said. 'Why do you say it like that?'

She picked up her cup of tea from the Rayburn.

'Well,' she said, 'Emma Tennant's father married his first wife in Wells Cathedral in 1925.'

'How on earth do you know that?' I said. I knew my grandmother had come from the tiny Somerset city. But I wasn't sure how my mother would know about a wedding in the year in which she herself was born.

She put her cup of tea back down and gave me that serene smile only my mother can give. It's the sort of all-knowing, do-you-think-I'm-stupid look that she does very well.

'Well,' she said. 'He married Pamela Paget. I was named after the bride.'

How many signs did anyone need?

So here we were, back in this Greek village to which the signs had directed us, and the sound of children at play once again wafting across from the primary school. The voices of children yelling in any language are much the same the world over. It reminded me of our Dorset village where we were about the same distance from the school. Strangely, in the heat and sunshine and spirit of adventure, I felt at home rather than homesick.

As my husband rifled through his suitcase for the house key, I went around from the back of the house to the front, intending to soak in the lovely views out across the village to the mountains. Only I couldn't see the mountains. They were obscured by skyscraper oleander bushes. Everywhere I looked, the garden was far more overgrown than I remembered. It had been pretty bad back in June. But now, it was dismal and dark; there was lichen growing on the cover of the swimming pool and the overhanging fronds of the palm tree were more lethal than any saw blade. Inside, the house which had been so lovely and homely when we saw it in June was now dusty and bare.

We unloaded the cars and took in our boxes and cases, piling them up in the hallway. And as we started putting things away it dawned on us that the whole place needed cleaning from top to bottom. There was mould crawling up the inside of the windows, grime instead of provisions in the kitchen cupboards and a wooden staircase which needed a damned good sweeping. I wouldn't have been surprised to open a door and find a Greek version of Miss Havisham sitting in the corner. My menopausal hormones kicked in and I began to weep. I sat on the packing cases, like Paddington Bear, wanting to go home.

Ever the pragmatist, my husband rummaged around in a box labelled 'drinks'.

'This'll cheer you up,' he said.

He pulled out a bottle of Dom Perignon, which had been given to us as a wedding present fourteen years earlier. This was our favourite travel tip and I have no hesitation in sharing it: if you're going away, always take a bottle of bubbly or decent wine with you. If the journey is hard and your destination is disappointing, at least you'll have something to drown your sorrows when you get there.

The champagne cork popped out just as it should, like a duchess breaking wind, and my husband poured the bubbly into magnificent, Mexican-style cocktail glasses which had come with us all the way from England and would never be used again over the next twelve months.

We chinked the glasses (but not too hard because we didn't want to break them) and raised a toast.

'*Yamas*,' my husband said. 'Here's to our big fat Greek gap year.'

Up in the village *plateia*, the old woman who had waved to us from the tavern ushered us to a sunny table for a late lunch at one of the tables outside. This was the oldest of the village's three tavernas and named after the owner, who told us in Greek that she was eighty-six. She introduced us to her twenty-something granddaughter, another Elizabeth, who shook our hands and, in excellent English, welcomed us to the village.

In the afternoon heat, our legs stuck to the plastic cover of the double seat. We changed tables as the smell of petrol from a broken-looking scooter propped up against the taverna wall wafted across and threatened to put us off our food. We ordered *pastitsada* – big hunks of beef cooked in a rich tomato sauce and served with thick spaghetti – and what was described as *Saganiki of Grandmother*, which turned out to be a huge omelette, with melted feta cheese and ham inside. The school bus, a purple twenty-seater with *Michaelis 1* emblazoned across the windscreen, struggled to get through; so we and the family on the next table got up from our chairs, breathed in and let it pass.

Just as we all settled back down to eat, two distracted dogs gambolled by. Their focus was a bitch on heat, a collie-cross-Alsatian with looks only a mother could love. Her pursuers were a handsome golden Labrador and a small, skinny, mangy creature which looked like a Muppet with a scabby head. The two dogs circled the female, which we quickly nicknamed Madam Cyn, and the Labrador made a half-hearted attempt at mating. And then another Labrador trotted up, with his tongue and more hanging out. He had a fatter, more determined head than his main love rival and wore a thick, studded collar. He aimed for the prize immediately, did the business and then bitch and dog were tied together like the Pushmi-pullyu from *Doctor Doolittle,* dragging each other up and down the street.

Young Elizabeth the waitress pouted as she saw us, cutlery poised and staring at the dogs.

'Animals are so free. It is natural,' she said, pouring out our wine.

The open-mouthed children on the next table had their eyes fixed on the dogs, ignoring attempts by their parents to engage them in conversation.

For a good half hour, the two dogs were joined together, panting and smiling and wagging their tails, with one long, joint body between them. The scabby-headed dog looked on wistfully before toddling off home, which turned out to be a shady spot next to the rubbish bins. It was closely followed by the first Labrador. Not long afterwards, a man in his fifties, with hardly any teeth, a shaved head topped by a tiny Mohican strip, and a pair of white plastic sunglasses on his forehead, strolled out from the taverna. He sat astride the clapped-out, petrol-smelling scooter and swore as he tried to get it going. He gave up, trundled it down the road and bump-started it.

'That,' Elizabeth the waitress said, with a look of disdain, 'is my father.'

Back at the Villa Oleander, replete with food and wine, I set about getting our bed ready for the night. I opened a wardrobe door and six lots of musty sheets fell on my head. I ferreted around in our boxes to find the washing powder and placed the bedding in the washing machine for a quick wash before putting it in the tumble drier. Blow the cost, needs must.

A pale ginger cat peered in at me from the terrace.

'You're not letting that thing in here,' my husband said, before I'd even had a chance to bond with it. I was still smarting at having to rehome our dogs for our year out.

'You do it with one, and the next minute there'll be hundreds in here.'

One thing Greece is not short of is stray cats and dogs.

That night, a fierce storm broke out, with thunder on the mountain. It sounded like Zeus playing a huge game of skittles in the sky, with all twelve Olympians on his team. Hephaestus, the blacksmith of the gods, had just knocked all the pins down in one go, which in our part of the south west is known as a *flopper*. After a lifetime, the storm died down and we tried to get some sleep. Twenty minutes later, dawn prised its rosy fingers through the thin curtains and all hell broke loose as more than a dozen cockerels began to yell across the village, closely followed by a gaggle of geese honking on the plot of land next door, a cacophony of barking dogs and then hunters shooting on the hillside. We pulled back the curtains and the sun fell over itself to greet us. The light streamed in through the windows, making the dust on them show up even more. And then we heard the schoolchildren outside, skipping by on their way to school. It was already eight o'clock and time to get up. This was to be the soundtrack to our lives each and every morning.

Devoid of sleep, I staggered out of bed to the en-suite bathroom and turned on the shower. The taps gurgled, coughed and spat, filling the bath with a muddy liquid that looked more like oxtail soup than water. I shrieked when I lifted the lid of the lavatory to see rust-coloured streaks in the pan.

'This bloody house!' I said as my husband came rushing in to see what was wrong. 'I'm sure it wasn't this bad when we saw it in June.'

'It's fine,' he said. 'It's cosmetic. We'll sort it, don't worry. A few soda crystals will get rid of the stains. If you keep the taps turned on, the water will come through clear, believe me.'

I was on my hands and knees cleaning the bathroom, wondering why I'd given up a really good job for this, when I heard my husband outside, talking to someone with a deep, gruff voice, like a box of rusty nails. It sounded like Anthony Quinn as Zorbas. It was a voice bigger than a gravelled drive.

'When him you want, you tell me,' the voice boomed. He called my husband Andreas – *An-dray-ass* - and the two of them were talking as if they'd known each other all their lives.

From the upstairs window, I could see a large, forty-something man on the doorstep with a little brown dog by his feet. He had a dark ponytail held in place by a red bandana. He wore jeans, his stomach spilling out from under a red tee-shirt.

He reminded me of Baloo the Bear from the Walt Disney film *The Jungle Book*.

'It is no problem, Andreas,' the bear growled, patting my husband on the shoulder. 'This afternoon I bring him.'

I went downstairs, curious to find out what was going on.

'This is Spiros, our neighbour, and his dog, Defa,' Andreas said.

The large man thrust out his hand. He could have crushed skulls with it. It was a solid, big handshake, like the man it came from. His name came as no surprise. Every family on the island had at least one Spiros, named after St Spyridon, the island's patron saint, whose ancient body lay in an ornate casket in the main church in Corfu Town.

'The house was built by Spiros' brother,' Andreas said, as I bent down to stroke the dog.

'Well,' I said to our new neighbour. 'Your brother built it very well.'

'Of course he build it well.' Spiros blocked the light into the house as he stood in the doorway. His voice came from his diaphragm but, at the same time, from the back of his throat. 'My brother, him is craftsman. Him is builder, like me.'

'Well, that's a useful person to have as a next door neighbour,' I said to Andreas as Spiros left, the little dog trotting behind him. 'So who's he bringing around this afternoon? His brother?'

'He's not bringing a person. He's bringing a chainsaw. He said he'll give me a hand to trim some of the trees in the garden.'

Up from the garden came the distinctive roar of a chainsaw as Spiros and Andreas, who followed the big man around like the sorcerer's apprentice, got to work. The garden wilderness became clearer and a neat pile of logs began to take shape next to the house. Already seasoned because most of the wood was dead, Spiros said it would be just right for the winter months ahead. And after cutting down the rotten trees and pruning the oleander, the view was just beautiful. It was worth a photo, with the wispy clouds lying below the mountain tops and the juxtaposition of red, terracotta and ochre roofs and walls clinging to the hillside, so I grabbed my camera and unhooked the mosquito screen covering the window. In an instant, the screen flew up and hit me in the eye, almost knocking me out. I was beginning to think the house had got it in for me.

Every day that week, we scrubbed, washed, dusted, polished and hoovered. As the days went on, my black eye faded and the Villa Oleander felt much fresher and cleaner. We tidied up to a soundtrack of 60s soul music, with Frank Wilson singing 'Do I Love You? ' and my husband shouting back: 'Indeed I do!' with his head down a lavatory as he attempted to descale it. The house smelled of wax polish and bleach and the cobwebs on the ceiling swayed to Tammi Terrell as she sang 'Two Can Have a Party'. Every now and then we thought we'd finished; and then I'd open a cupboard to find something else needed doing. But we were not despondent. It was the Blitz spirit and we were in this together.

November

The village sits on the side of a mountain, its houses tumbling down towards the valley floor. The modest buildings, some of them old, others modern, cluster around a central *plateia*, with three tavernas – Dukas, Elizabeth's and To Steki - on the north side, a community hall to the west with the water board office above it, a church to the east, and a mini-market and *kafenio* to the south. A Greek village would not be complete without a *kafenio*, that traditional male bastion where the men play cards, drink coffee, watch television and put the world to rights while the women are busy at home.

In the middle of the *plateia* are two small trees, a water fountain, a telephone booth to one side and an assortment of tables and chairs, set out by the owners of the *kafenio* for people to sit on. There is a war memorial next to the church for all the countrymen who died during Greece's many struggles with enemy forces. The memorial is surrounded by a small picket fence and gate, which is left open most of the time but remained closed in the days after 28 October when it was decorated with national flags for *Oxi* Day, a date marked by Greeks all over the world. It was on this day in 1941 that Greece entered World War II after Prime Minister Metaxas said no (*oxi*) to Mussolini's ultimatum to allow the Italian army free passage to enter and occupy strategic sites in Greece.

Narrow alleyways radiate from the village centre, like a jellyfish with lots of tentacles. The surrounding hills give the village a kind of amphitheatre effect, with the few people dotted around and walking through its streets actors on a stage. Gazing down on the *plateia* is an imposing building with crenulations and odd-shaped windows. Spiros told us it belonged to the Theotokis family who, in years gone by, were prominent politicians in Greece. The building was empty now, but for a solitary caretaker and three loud dogs.

In the *plateia*, a bug-eyed cat scampered towards me, desperate for scraps and a bit of love. From inside the *kafenio*, my husband signalled to me to find out what I wanted to drink. I went in to join him at the counter, passing two old men sitting outside who nodded when I greeted them in clumsy Greek.

The *kafenio* comprised a room with a tiled floor and lots of small tables and chairs. It was just after five-thirty and the only people around were the young woman behind the counter and two children in the mini-market, which was at the side and rear of the same *kafenio*. This part of the interior was jam-packed with shelves and refrigerators selling a variety of produce: sacks of dried beans, local wine in water bottles, fresh bread, cheese, household goods, notebooks and lucky bags for the children. It was like an English shop from the 1960s, with the most unlikely things jostling for pole position on the shelves.

The woman behind the counter introduced herself. A cheerful blonde aged about thirty-five, she told us her name was Kiki and explained that her family ran the place. We were about to launch ourselves into the 'we're living here for a year' speech when a steady flow of men began to enter the *kafenio*, picking up pieces of paper and packs of cards from the counter and settling down at the tables. Others drew up chairs to watch as the games began. Sitting at the corner of the bar, I felt as if I didn't belong, the barbarian Medea, a foreign female putting a jinx on the game. I said as much to Kiki.

'You stay,' Kiki said. 'We are okay.'

She plopped two large glass beakers of local wine down onto the counter: one white, one dark red.

'These are on me,' she said. 'Welcome to our village.'

'Thank you,' Andreas said. 'But you're very naughty.'

'Always naughty.' She gave a toss of her head and a conspiratorial smile.

Over the next few evenings, I sat in the corner of the *kafenio*, watching and listening with awe as the men slapped their cards onto the tables, gabbling in raised voices when they felt hard done by and going outside every now and then for a smoke. Some of the older ones bowed out, to be replaced by young men in their twenties with grown-out Mohican-style haircuts. Kiki bustled around, efficient and polite, but she was not one to take orders. She was serving but not a servant. She was definitely in charge.

One evening, the door opened and a middle-aged man with longish, grey hair and wearing double-denim strolled in, his lips pursed around a cigarette. The theme tune to *The Good, The Bad and The Ugly* ran through my head. Kiki yelled and the man was back out again in a flash, taking a few last drags on his cigarette outside the door before putting it out and coming back in again. Unlike so many other places where Greeks completely ignored smoking bans, this place was definitely a nicotine-free zone, especially with Kiki behind the counter.

On the spot, I nicknamed the double-denim man Flash and then realised I would need names for all of these people. Over the next few days, and with Kiki's help, I built up quite a cast list comprising real names and epithets as an aide memoire. If epithets were good enough for Homer, they were sure as hell good enough for me. So instead of the wanderer Odysseus and Menelaus, the red-haired king of Sparta, there was Turkey Spiros, so called because he owed the turkeys in the olive groves, Spiros Paleo who worked in Paleokastritsa, Spiros Waiter who worked in the Taverna Dukas, Spiros Ron who looked like an older, smaller version of my husband's brother, Ron, and Spiros Runner who always wore bright trainers and ran errands for the *kafenio*. There was our own neighbour, who we called Spiros Bear because of his strength; Alekos the schoolteacher; Lovejoy the builder; Kostas the Albanian; Kostas Leather Hat; the waitress Elizabeth's father, Yannis of the Mohican and Clapped-out Scooter; an old man called Theodoros who I named Matt Monro because of his beaming, broad face and his way with a song; Nikos the Moustache; a man we knew as Dave because he looked like my son's friend; Smiling Ilias and Big Nikos, an accountant who appeared to have a different tracksuit for each night of the week. As we got to know the village, the cast list grew.

In the *kafenio* each night, the hubbub grew louder and louder, cards slapping and the two professionals – the school teacher and the accountant – making the most noise, as if to announce their superiority. The door would swing open again and all would go quiet as Elizabeth, the waitress from the taverna,

41

entered stage left and pouted before selecting onions and potatoes for the night's menu. She always left with a confident swagger.

It quickly became clear to me, from my eyrie in the corner, that although this might appear to be a man's world, it was the women who did most of the work.

We were tolerated during those evenings but no-one, apart from Kiki, ever spoke to us. Our lack of Greek was a nuisance. We could do the basics but as soon as anyone expanded on that, we were flummoxed. But we made a pact to smile sweetly at people and wish them good day in Greek as best we could.

The cats patrolled the rubbish skips on the corner of our road. In every village you saw them, guarding their spoils. At every skip and wheelie bin, there was a cat, guarding its territory. A large ginger one, a tortoiseshell which was surprisingly fluffy given the climate, numerous black and white ones and the odd fat tabby, one with a stubby tail and another with a weird eye. Nobody wanted them.

Down in Paleokastritsa, the monastery donkey wandered unhindered by traffic or holidaymakers, clattering up the steps to the Apollon Hotel for a change of scenery. In the valley, the dogs barked, setting off a chain reaction among hounds and mongrels chained up outside what looked more like shacks than houses. The geese honked and turkeys scuttled through the olive groves.

It was November but still the peacock butterflies fluttered by. In the evening, the smoke of a dozen bonfires lay low across the plain, like ribbons of mist. It was a glorious place, this village, and I was determined to make the most of my year away. I would soak up this atmosphere and beauty and get on with writing projects which had been left unfinished for too long. A spell had been woven and, slowly and surely, our new home was turning into a Greek version of what we had left behind in Dorset. I refused to let the homesickness eat me up. I would not get irritated by my husband every other minute. I would stop wishing I was back home in cold and wet England. I was extraordinarily lucky, I kept telling myself.

I could do this.

In the market in Corfu Town, the stalls were full of wild greens – *xorta* – spinach and cucumbers for four for a euro. There was calamari at fourteen euros a kilo, John Dory at fifteen and giant prawns at eighteen. In the butchers' shops there were lamb chops, beef steak, pork and *sheftalia* for those in the know.

In the UK, snow was falling. Here in Corfu, every day we opened our windows to sunshine coming up around the mountain. Our mornings were broken by the cockadoodledooing of a dozen cockerels, whose constant cries punctuated the coming of the day. Their persistent yells set off the dogs, then the geese and then the turkeys. And on Sundays the church bells clanged a dreadful tune which even Hades, the god of the underworld, would not recognise. How the dogs howled then.

Later, the pigeons flapped in the citrus trees, chainsaws buzzed in the distance, wood was chopped and Andreas pruned the palm.

On Sundays, we would sit down at the Taverna Dukas next to the *plateia* where we would feast on pork in the oven and roast potatoes, eyed enviously by the bug-eyed cat and a wire-haired hunting dog with mange. The taverna was the recommendation of Spiros Bear, who had run his own taverna a few years ago in Paleokastritsa and knew his stuff. On our first outing, we dispensed with the menu and asked Spiros Waiter what was good. He brought us a large plate of thickly-sliced pork studded with garlic and surrounded by a mass of oily potatoes. It was salty, garlicky, oily, tender, sweet, moist and succulent. It oozed flavour and, having had it once, on Sunday mornings we were salivating by eleven o'clock in expectation of what to come. On our third visit, the pork had run out and we felt bereft, robbed, deprived, only to be brought to our knees by the alternative, the biggest portion of rooster *pastitsada* we had ever seen or attempted to eat. The rooster was meaty and full of flavour in a wild and rustic sauce that seeped into the fat spaghetti beneath. There was far too much, so we were given a doggy bag to take home after we had finished our complementary glasses of limoncello and plate of Greek yoghurt and honey to share.

Spiros Waiter's grin spread across his face like a letterbox as he touched Andreas on the shoulder. 'Your shirt. It is Gant,' he said, making a whooshing noise through his teeth. 'Very nice. And your watch, Mr Andrew, it is very nice.'

He pulled back his sleeve to compare his own Timberland watch with my husband's.

'It is nice. How much? You get me one when you next go to England?' Spiros Waiter said. 'I pay you.'

Spiros was a man obsessed with designer labels. It was said he had worked in the best restaurant in Greece and had acquired a taste for the high life.

On Remembrance Sunday, smartly-dressed visitors gathered in the British Cemetery for the laying of wreaths to remember the Corfu Channel incident of 1946 when the destroyers HMS *Saumarez* and HMS *Volage* struck mines in the water between the island and Albania. Some forty-four men were killed and forty-two injured.

Standing there in the lush cemetery, witnessing *Reveille* and the *Last Post* and the laying of wreaths, we could have been right back home. The cemetery was an oasis of green shade and calm, right next to the island's prison. It is lovingly tended by George Psailas, as it was by his father before him. He has a plot set aside for himself when the inevitable happens, right in the corner so he can still keep an eye on the cemetery when he has long gone.

Britishness is very much a part of Corfu, which is a place shaped by its past. There are echoes of archaic Greek, Classical and Byzantium as well as more recent influences from France and Britain. From the Venetians, Corfu got its olive groves, masses of them, the swathes of pale green punctuated by groups of cypress trees, standing to attention like exclamation mark soldiers, giving perspective to the landscape.

The Venetians also made their mark on the architecture, with Corfu's old streets much like Venice but without the canals. Every now and then, in villages across the island, set up in the hills far away from marauders, you will see an arch, a doorway, a set of windows or a whole façade which screams out the island's Venetian heritage.

And then there were the French, who gave the island the Liston, under whose stylish edifice my husband and I sealed the deal on our year away.

And then there was the British protectorate from 1814 to 1864, which gave Corfu ginger beer and cricket. It was during this time that the island's first philharmonic band came into existence. For an island just sixty kilometres long and thirty kilometres wide, it's hard to believe that Corfu has eighteen philharmonic orchestras. They come out on high days and holidays, parading around the town and filling the streets with the sound of their rousing marches.

But although the island is sixty miles from the heel of Italy and shaped like an upside down Britain or a French can-can dancer's leg, shaking provocatively away from the mainland, it is first and foremost Greek. Known as Kerkyra by the Greeks, its name is said to come from the nymph Korkyra, who was abducted by Poseidon and brought to the island which he named for her. The Italians called it Corfu.

The lovely island sits in Homer's wine-dark Ionian Sea and is the gateway to Greece. With an abundance of rain in the winter and sun in the summer, it's green and fertile and known as The Garden Isle. It has four million olive trees and so many wild flowers, including forty-five different species of orchids.

My husband had known Corfu since the Sixties when, with his family, he stayed as a child at the Hotel Potamaki in Benitses. As a couple, we had been coming here for more than ten years. I had just studied ancient magic and, of the ten Greek islands I had visited, Corfu was the one that cast its spell. Its glorious mix of influences, combined with its *Greekness*, made for a very special, heady concoction.

The island has long been a magnet for British travellers, from the moneyed classes in the north east to the lager lout brigade down south in Kavos. There are holiday resorts dotted all along the coast, north, east and west. There are many who believe it's been spoiled by tourism, the scourge being the all-inclusive hotels. But it's easy to get away from it all, on secret beaches undiscovered by the masses and in the hillside villages hidden from the tourist trail, where the cypress trees wisp up through the olive groves towards the mountainside and then tumble back down again into the clear azure sea. For every kiss-me-quick seaside resort – and there really aren't many like that – there are a dozen villages tucked away from the hordes, beating to their

45

own drums. Ours was one of them. We were set back in the foothills of the mountains just five minutes' drive from Paleokastritsa, a popular resort with five bays of crystal-clear water. But, rather like our home in Dorset, a short car journey away from the world-famous Jurassic Coast, our village was just far enough away from the madding crowd. It was how we liked it.

It was the end of the season and the holidaymakers had packed up and gone home. Direct flights would, for the winter months at least, be a thing of the past and we would need to go via Athens if we wanted to get back to Dorset. Most tavernas were closed, with tables and chairs stacked up in the corners. In Corfu's old town, a UNESCO world heritage site, gift shops were shut and the pace throughout the whole island became much slower. Even the boy racers had stopped racing.

The smell of wood smoke from bonfires replaced the sweet and sour smell of old drains. Nets were beginning to be laid out beneath the olive trees, in case the precious fruit dropped before the harvest. As in the UK, the clocks went back at the end of October. We were still two hours ahead but it got darker much earlier. The sea, though, was still warm. At Paleokastritsa, our nearest beach, the waves rose and fell gently over the shingle. There was not a soul to be seen in the clear water, apart from us and the occasional jellyfish, which I discovered only after it had stung me.

Autumn and winter were times for exploration. Down through the island, along a back road purporting to be something bigger, the smoke from bonfires wisped up into a crisp, blue sky as people cleared the ground below the olive trees in preparation for the harvest. A middle-aged woman with a strimmer waved to an older man with a small truck full of clippings. The smell of autumn was in the air, although the days were warm and, for us, hot enough to swim. Lefkimmi, Corfu's second town, dozed. By the river, the mullet swished along the murky water in front of the closed-up tavernas. An old widow in black, with a scarf on her head for protection from the sun, could barely walk in her garden when standing. But, on her hands and knees with a hoe, she made good progress in cleaning the soil.

The southern part of the island is a place where some rarely venture. Indeed, a guidebook I found on the bookshelf of the Villa Oleander declared there was nothing down here of any interest. And for some time, having spent holidays only in the north of the island, I had believed this to be true. But now, as a local, I was able to see for myself the long, sandy beaches, the undulating countryside full of olive groves and little villages. An ancient castle, beautiful lakes. To say the south of the island was not worth visiting was a blatant lie. I wondered if the author had shares in tourist property in the north. I was beginning to see that Corfu had something for every kind of visitor. For me, drawn to history both ancient and modern, beautiful landscape, delicious food and wonderfully hospitable people, the island had it all.

Back in Lefkimmi, young men sitting in leather and raffia chairs drank iced coffee in an incongruous cafe bar, looking out across an odd architectural mix. A police 4 x 4 cruised up and down the street and over the bridge and back again, looking for Lefkimmi Vice. There was none, now that the young Brits had deserted Kavos, that fleshpot fake, that sin city strip a few kilometres away, where teenagers were reputed to drink each other's urine and to shag anything that moved. This was the Corfu that didn't interest me; but in November, Kavos was fascinating, like a deserted outpost in the Wild West when the gold rush was over. Everything was closed. The empty main street, flanked by nightclubs and bars called Buzz, Madison and Future, Rolling Stone, a shop called Bulldog Tattoos and the omnipresent McDonald's, was a shadow of its former summer self. Where on hot summer nights teenage boys celebrated their GCSE results by synchronised mooning while the girls got their breasts out, now there was nothing, not even a tumbleweed trainer or a fleeing flip-flop to suggest they were ever there.

Up in the north at our favourite taverna, The Three Brothers in Astrakeri, the proprietor's son – who I called Yanni Pianni because of his prowess for playing romantic ballads on the piano

– pulled up a chair after serving us with his mother's octopus in red sauce and *xorta*. It was a dish I had tried all over Greece and, in the thirteen years I had been visiting the country, his mother, Aleki, definitely served the best. Tender, succulent octopus in a rich sauce. It was my favourite meal in the whole wide world.

'So, how does it feel to be here for a whole year?' he said. 'It is very beautiful, yes?'

Looking out over the small harbour and the sandy beach, across to the Corfu Channel with Albania seeming so close you could touch it, was a sight of which I would never tire.

But, still, I so missed home.

Part II

Winter

'Love is a temporary madness, it erupts like volcanoes and then subsides. And when it subsides, you have to make a decision. You have to work out whether your roots have so entwined together that it is inconceivable that you should ever part.
Because this is what love is.'

Louis de Bernières, *Captain Corelli's Mandolin*

December

There was a chill in the air, as if the wind was blowing from the Russian Steppes or the Caucasus or wherever cold weather came from at this time of year. Piles of logs were stacked outside people's houses and, in the afternoons, smoke rose from people's chimneys as fires were lit inside. Those who visited Corfu only in the summer season would never believe how cold, damp and wet it is in winter. There is a reason why the island is so green.

On rainy days, the water burst from the sky like it had come from a newly-discovered spring. It turned roads into rivers in an instant. In the streets of Corfu's Old Town, the rain fell in straight lines, like great exclamation marks. The water rushed down from the Liston, past St Spyridon's Church and down, down, past the colonnades and around the corner towards the Spilia. There was a tremendous flash and a tumultuous crash as thunder and lightning hit the island's capital. When it rained in Corfu, it really rained. Not a snivel, a drivel, just unrelenting stair-rods smashing on to the pavements until, within seconds, it became a stream.

And then the rain died down and there was bright, white sunshine.

We had been here two months and, despite the beauty and magic of this place, I could not get Dorset out of my head. There was a real ache in my bones and in my heart, in my whole being. I loved the Corfu countryside but I longed to see the lush, slushy fields back home and walk through them with my granddaughter. I really hadn't thought I was going to feel like this. I was cross with myself. Here I was, doing something others would give an arm and a leg to do, in a country where people were suffering, really suffering, and I felt sorry for myself because I didn't want to be here. At the same time, I was becoming increasingly irritated with Andreas who, being married to a menopausal, formerly independent woman, was bearing the brunt of my moods. I reasoned we were here on this gap year for the sake of Andreas's health, so it was his fault I was feeling so low. I had conveniently forgotten how I'd jumped at the chance earlier in the year and how it was I who had organised all the property viewings in Corfu. Now reality was here, in the shape of thunder and lightning outside, a log fire inside and draughts coming in from under the front door. At times like this, I could just as well have been in England. But I was stuck with it because we had just had a phone call to say our house in Dorset had been let. It was good news really. It meant we had money coming in, rather than just Andreas's pension. But it also meant I couldn't go back. The umbilical cord had been cut, at least until the autumn of next year.

One day, a dark and dismal day in Corfu Town, he insisted on gripping my arm tightly before we crossed the road, telling me when it was safe to do so. In recent weeks, this had been becoming a habit. He would frequently put his hand out in front of me, like my mother used when she was driving in the days before seat belts, to stop me from falling forward. He was being protective, keeping me safe, but I just wanted to stab him.

'Where are we going?' I said, as we made our way up an unfamiliar side street off the busy San Rocco Square.

'I need to get some cornflour.' He was obsessed with food, obsessed with cooking. It's not a bad thing, I know, but now that he was retired he had more time to do it and I never got a look in. And there were days when I would have been quite happy having a break from the writing and the homesickness to do a bit of prepping in the kitchen. Cooking is a form of therapy; it could keep me on the move when I was flagging, fill me with anticipation of what I was creating. But when someone else is in charge and you no longer have that activity, you feel as though something has been taken away from you. I had already given up my job. It was as if another part of me, the homemaker, was also redundant.

'What do you want cornflour for?' I asked. He hadn't divulged what his latest dish was going to be.

'It's a thickening agent,' he said.

I knew what cornflour was. I used to cook once.

If that morning I had been carrying a *souvlaki* skewer, Andreas would have found it sticking out the back of his hand, preferably the one he used most for cooking. Familiarity breeds contempt. I was beginning to appreciate that this must be how some newly-retired couples felt. Resentment was building up inside me like a pressure cooker.

It probably didn't help us going back to the UK for a week, just a few months after arriving in Corfu. But that was what we did, to take Christmas presents to the family.

It was as if we had never been away.

At the Christmas bazaar in our village hall, our friends and neighbours wore Santa hats and baubles and fought over each other to give us a hug.

'It's so nice to see you,' said one of the loveliest ladies in the village, giving me a playful prod in the back.

With Andreas up in Bristol watching a football match, I was without a car so travelled into Bridport by bus for the first time ever. I stood, freezing cold, at the village bus stop as customers from the bazaar went past, loaded with cakes, raffle prizes they didn't really want and bags full of home-made pasties for the freezer. On the bus journey, the heaters blew out welcome warm air as I gazed from the windows out over the beautiful countryside of West Dorset. It was a perfect, crisp, winter's day, with a sky of blue and a magical light. When the bus finally rattled into town, I almost kissed the pavement as I got off outside the NatWest. The Christmas trees had been put up above the shops and a string of lights had been installed across the street near the town hall. I was happy to be home and wanted to run down the streets like a child in a superhero's outfit. But my first port of call was a shop where I could buy a woolly hat to cover my cold ears.

And then the next day when I went to get my hair cut in Beaminster – a town so quiet since the tunnel closed after the fatal landslip back in the summer – a rainbow arched over the town square. I took it as a symbol of hope, perhaps, for good times on the horizon, not just for Beaminster but also, selfishly, for me. And then I saw my children, the grandchildren, the siblings, my parents, my cats; and Andreas said to me: 'You don't want to go back to Corfu, do you?' And it was true, I didn't. I would have been quite happy if he had left me in Dorset and returned on his own.

We touched down in Corfu in the rain. After picking up our luggage from the carousel, we walked in silence through the lobby and out into the evening air. The place looked distant and dark as I pressed my face against the taxi window. I could see nothing but unfamiliar shadows and rain. Back at the house, we dumped our cases and walked in overcoats and hats up to the *kafenio*. The old men sat smoking in the *plateia* while inside, young men were engrossed in a card game with Spiros Waiter. Kiki's brother, Tasso the baker, was stacking the mini-market shelves. On television, Panathinaikos and Tottenham Hotspur battled it out in the Europa League while the youngsters slapped the cards down loudly on the marble-topped tables and yelled *malakas* at each other. In walked Flash, the ageing rocker in double-denim and with a hairstyle from the 1970s. The ever-cheerful Kiki came out from behind the counter to embrace us. Her radiance was infectious. I couldn't help but smile.

She handed us a box of cakes bought to mark Nikos the accountant's name day and asked us to take our pick.

'We are okay?' she asked. Before we even had a chance to nod, she went back behind the counter to pour us a drink. 'It is lovely to see you back. And you look more beautiful than before.'

Spiros Waiter looked up from his cards and peered out from over his red plastic spectacles.

'Welcome, welcome,' he said, nodding and making a *sheesh* noise as he contorted his face to reveal his teeth in a wide grin. 'Did you get the watch, Andreas?'

Andreas produced a bag for Spiros Waiter and handed it over. His smile threatened to knock over the display of Christmas *kourabiedes* and *melomakarona* biscuits from the table next to the counter.

Kiki put two filo pies into a bag 'on the house' for our breakfast and pushed them our way, refusing to accept payment.

'Kiki…'

'Always naughty,' she said.

54

We found a couple of stools at the bar. There was such a hubbub here and so many smiling faces, I now felt guilty for not wanting to come back. Because that evening in Corfu, it seemed as if we had come home.

We sat down at *To Steki*, Spirodoula's taverna on the corner, to a hearty beef *stifado* – hunks of slow-cooked beef in a rich, dark red sauce with button onions. On our way home we were passed by Madam Cyn, the bitch we had seen getting all the attention outside *Elizabeth's Taverna* back in October. She was heavily pregnant and looking for a place to bed down and have her pups.

There was a familiar figure down in the olive groves. Spiros Bear, in red boiler suit and matching bandana, was hard at work with his Russian girlfriend Natalia by his side and the dog Defa at his feet. They were sifting through the olives that had blown onto the ground prior to the harvest in the new year.

'What you doing?' Spiros said, stopping to light a cigarette.

We explained we were on a walk so that we could see the village from different angles.

'What you doing tomorrow?' he asked.

We had nothing planned at all.

'You come to my house. It is my name day.'

Name days in Greece are more important than birthdays. I had once asked Dimitris, the son of our friend Gorgeous George, if he envied his brothers Aeneas and Paris for their romantic and ancient Greek names. In the *Iliad*, it's Paris who sparks the Trojan War by abducting Helen. In *Aeneid*, Virgil's Latin epic poem, it is Aeneas who escapes from Troy after it has been sacked by the Greeks and goes on to found ancient Rome.

Dimitris thought for a minute. Maybe he would like to have been called Hector or Achilles?

'Yes, I do envy them,' he said.

I knew as much. If my sisters had been called Penelope and Ariadne, I would have felt short-changed if I'd been given the name Susan.

'I envy them because they *don't* have name days,' he said. 'They never have to buy the drinks or the cakes.'

So much for Greek hospitality.

55

In Corfu, St Spyridon is the most important saint of all. He had twice saved the island from the Turks and once from the plague. The day would be a bank holiday as Corfiots celebrated their patron, so the prospect of sharing part of it with Spiros Bear felt like an honour.

In the morning, the church bells clanged at just before eight o'clock and then again just before nine. Spiros' little dog, Defa, yapped in excitement as her master fired up the wood oven outside and stoked up the coals under the grill.

'See you later,' he said, as we took the car into Corfu Town. Outside the Church of St Spyridon, where the saint's eighteen-hundred-year-old body is kept in a highly decorated casket, it was standing room only. The devoted and curious pushed their way in to see and hear and smell the splendour of the service in the golden, candlelit interior. The small gift shops next to the church were doing a roaring trade, selling candles, icons and worry beads. Stalls nearby, manned by minor holy men, received a steady trickle of customers while the doughnut stands were even busier. At the main entrance to the church, a beautiful beggar woman and her two children were handed bread torn off from rolls given to the congregation.

The children gorged on plastic cups filled with pine nuts, sultanas, walnuts, sesame seeds and pomegranate. Bay leaves crunched underfoot. A woman in sunglasses and fur jacket walked arm-in-arm with a man in a dark overcoat, who was talking loudly into his mobile phone. A man in a Santa hat and an old lady with a headscarf loitered around the door to the saint's shrine, hoping to get in as the VIPs came out.

The priest's song inside the church was amplified to the people outside, who bought candles for the dead and lottery tickets for themselves. Bells clanged as the service came to an end and those lucky enough to have squeezed inside spilled out of the main entrance. The beggar woman was given a disdainful look by a policeman smoking a long cigarette. He tolerated her until his senior officer, a handsome man in a dashing uniform, told him to move the woman and the children on.

There was a swish of black robe, and a long black-grey beard. A priest walked by and handed the beggar children some sweets.

For the pigeons on the buildings opposite, it was just another day. Soon, they would swoop down for the crumbs and seeds.

Back in the village, smoke rose from Spiros Bear's chimney. Pork on the rotisserie grill dribbled luscious fat onto the coals below while baked feta bubbled away in the oven and beef cooked slowly in a rich sauce. Defa the dog lay on the doormat as twenty of us sat round two tables joined together in an L shape in Spiros' kitchen. The table was laden with grilled pork, beef *pastitsada*, coleslaw, beetroot and potato salad, red, white and rose wine made by various guests and Ribena for Spiros who didn't drink alcohol. He went round the table, introducing us to his brother Lambis, sister Koula, who we realised was the woman we had seen with the goats as we drove into the village on our first day, and her husband, Ilias. There were other members of the family and friends, including a vivacious blonde woman called Betty, a Hungarian who was married to Spiros' nephew and had her hands full supervising two small children. She was fluent in English and Greek and, every now and then, would translate for us as the native language gabbled around our ears like a rushing waterfall, hands flying out across the table to gesticulate, pour out wine and pick up food.

'You must have my mother's wine, Andreas,' her husband Antonis said, with an ironic smile as he poured out two small glasses for us. 'It is very good. Koula make it from your grapes last year.'

Andreas downed his glass in one. I'm not sure if it was my imagination but I could swear I saw a slight green tinge to his face. I sipped my wine delicately. When no-one was looking, I discreetly pushed my glass to one side.

It was terrible.

'You like, Andreas?'

Andreas nodded, just to be polite.

'Here,' Antonis said. 'You can have bottle to take home.'

Roars of laughter went around the table. The food consumed and stomachs full, Spiros offered Andreas a cigarette.

'You smoke, Andreas?'

He didn't.

'Only after sex,' he replied.

57

I was embarrassed, and there was an uneasy silence as Betty did a quick translation. And then the laughter rippled around the room like a Mexican wave, accompanied by loud gabbling in Greek. Andreas got up from his chair, raised his glass of wine and declared: '*Yamas!*' A few minutes later, Spiros' brother-in-law Ilias did the same.

'*Yamas!*' everyone yelled. And that was it; we had been taken under the wing of a remarkable family. Being the youngest of five, I should have felt pretty good about it.

As we walked out of the house, Andreas turned around and invited them all to our house for 'nibbles and drinks' on the Sunday before Christmas.

'What are you looking at me like that for?' he said, as we walked through the gate and into our house.

'You could have asked me first.'

I reasoned that would have been the polite thing to have done. The reality was that I was trying to pick a fight with him. He'd been the centre of attention and was now revelling in it, arranging for another social event to confirm his position as the King of Corfu. I wanted him to shout back to give me a reason to feel mad at him.

'Well, we always have a house full at Christmas,' he said, stroking my arm. 'I thought it would make you feel more at home.'

I should have been thankful really. He was trying his best. I was just being a shrew. I have read somewhere that homesickness often goes deeper than missing a place or a person. What I was missing was a different version of myself. I was no longer independent, I was lacking in confidence because I couldn't speak the language. I couldn't play the fool and fit in with these people like Andreas just had. So I blamed him for my shortcomings. He was the reason why we were here. And when things were difficult, it was his fault. I knew I had to overcome these feelings and channel my energy into something other than self-pity. But it was hard, I tell you; bloody hard.

In the red-domed church of St Spyridon, there was a surge as a priest allowed the people to move forward one step at a time. A man refilled the incense burners in the ornate candelabra above the heads of the crowd as the security guard from Brinks held the ladder. The saint's casket had been open to view for the past three days and still they came to worship, from all over the world.

We queued up with the rest, scrunching the bay leaves underfoot, as a low rail funnelled the devoted towards the casket, which stood upright in front of the iconostasis, the ornate screen in front of the altar which is such a dominant feature in Greek Orthodox churches. The faithful were there to kiss the slippered feet of the ancient body of St Spyridon. Once a year, his upright casket is opened up at the foot end for a ritual which draw people to Corfu from all around the world. I steeled myself for what lay ahead, as my turn came to pay my respects to the saint, who was born only two hundred years or so after Jesus. The thought of a body that old and all those people who had been in that space spreading their germs before me was enough to make me want to escape. But it was no good, I was hemmed in. There was no turning back. When confronted with the eighteen-hundred-year-old feet, I bowed my head and did an air kiss above his woollen slippers. I stood up straight to look at his face, enclosed in a glass section of the casket. With his head at an acute angle and mouth open, he seemed rather uncomfortable. On the way out, I shuddered as we passed St Spyridon's hand encased in a silver box.

The veneration of holy relics has a long tradition in the Eastern Orthodox and Catholic Churches. As someone brought up as a no-frills Anglican, it both intrigued and baffled me. St Spyridon gets a new pair of socks knitted each year. Pieces of the old ones are cut up and handed out to the needy. Having been in contact with those ancient tarsals and metatarsals, the socks must have special powers. To my mind, it was not much different to having a magic charm such as a talisman, a lucky rabbit's foot or a pendant against the evil eye, but one given religious and spiritual significance by association. Still, each to their own. I could respect the beliefs of others even if I didn't share them.

'Well,' Andreas said, as we emerged into the bright sunshine. 'Did you kiss his feet?' He confessed that he had also avoided direct contact.

I had read in Gerald Durrell's *My Family and Other Animals* how the author's sister, Margo, had become ill after kissing the saintly slippers in an effort to cure her acne. I hoped our encounter with the saint would bode rather better for us than that.

I woke at three that morning, feeling very sick and unable to get warm. Being so close to St Spyridon's ancient feet had obviously done me no good at all. Andreas lit a fire and I snuggled under a blanket on the sofa, completely washed out. I turned to a thick book I had taken down from the shelf earlier in the week, never thinking I would have the time to read it. It was written by an American who had lived in the village for a decade during the 1970s. It was not long before I realised that the people he was writing about were the family of our own Spiros Bear. I was hooked and read it all at one sitting.

The next day I woke up feeling brighter and much better informed about the village, although my stomach still wasn't right. I had finished the book and was pleased to have been spoon-fed information, much of it going back hundreds of years, which would have taken me months to find out on my own. Maybe there was something in the magic healing powers of St Spyridon's feet after all. If I hadn't been ill, I would never have bothered to read the book.

It was several months into our adventure and I was still trying to convince myself that what we were doing was for the greater good, even if I was having trouble adapting. We were approaching Christmas, a time for family and friends. For the first time ever, I would be without them, and the thought kept turning and turning over in my head. The Christmas 'at home' was getting nearer, prompting Andreas to go into town for another shopping expedition. He was away from the house for five-and-a-half hours.

How long did it take to shop for food?

I got my phone out of my bag to text him.

'Bored now,' I wrote.

He texted back.

'Go and see your friend Kiki.'

I couldn't. I had a bad stomach, which suited my martyrdom. She also had a shop and *kafenio* to run. Why should she have to entertain a whining Brit?

'You poor thing,' I told myself. 'Here's your husband, having fun, doing one of the things he loves best – food shopping – and you're at home in a country you don't want to be in.'

I laid it on thick to myself, with a trowel. I was the only one who seemed to be listening.

In the village, Madam Cyn had her puppies, the ones conceived on our first day here. She had nestled down under the exterior staircase of a British woman's house and given birth to seven bouncing babies. I wondered what these pups would look like, having been there at the moment of conception. We paid for our coffee at the *kafenio* and walked down one of the many narrow alleyways that led off from the *plateia* to find them. But we were too late. The puppies had already gone, along with the mother, taken to a life of safety by an animal rescue charity. They were the lucky ones. It seemed that every other week a new stray dog found its way in to the village. It was something I would never get used to.

In the garden, the leaves of the citrus tree prunings crackled on the bonfire as the branches burned. Spiros Bear fired up his chainsaw and more overgrown oleander bit the dust. I had downed tools, at least for the time being, after being impaled on a palm spike. Inside, I nursed a swollen leg and cursed my luck. A black eye from a mosquito net, a jellyfish sting and now assault by palm frond. It was as if the natural world, the thing I set so much store by, was trying to tell me something. Like 'go home', perhaps.

It was time to read another book.

There were no letterboxes in our village doors. If we wanted anything sent to us, we had to have it addressed care of the mini-market and *kafenio*. The upside was that there was no junk mail littering the doormat each morning. As well as a cardboard box in the *kafenio* that anyone could leaf through, there was also a series of locked post boxes under the arches next to the community hall. For a price, you could rent one and have your post delivered free from prying eyes. We would sit outside the *kafenio* sometimes, watching the world go by. One morning, we saw the postman arrive in his white van. He took a large parcel and a briefcase full of mail to the *kafenio*. A stray dog padded up to us, and posed for a photo before giving himself a hearty scratch around the ears. The bug-eyed cat stared as we drank our coffee.

The old man at the next table was devoid of teeth but his walking stick looked capable of giving a nasty bite. He lashed out at the dog, which had taken a shine to anyone who slid a glance his way. The animal was too young to distinguish between friend and foe and gave everyone a chance. The old man's stick failed to make contact and the dog jogged on.

We had a ringside seat as the postman ambled out of the *kafenio* towards the mailboxes in the wall of the building opposite. He posted the envelopes in the various slots and then went to fetch the letters from the village's outgoing box: Christmas cards for nephews and nieces and grandchildren destined for mantelpieces all over the world.

A middle-aged man in work boots opened mailbox number six-five-zero-three, tore open one white envelope and ripped the letter inside up in an instant, putting the tiny pieces in the rubbish bin.

Another final demand.

The cost of electricity in Greece was about to go up by more than thirty per cent.

Up got the old man with the stick. He had been walking along this street every day for the past week. And once again, his mailbox was empty. The card he was expecting from the son in Australia he would never see again had still not arrived.

We needed to cheer the house up and make it feel more Christmassy. I was damned if I was going to wallow in a pool of self-pity for ever. I was not some whining American. I needed to pull myself together. Some tinsel and bright lights would be enough to change my mood, at least temporarily. We drew the line at paying seventy euros for a small Christmas tree from a garden centre, so we improvised by decorating a bare branch of a daphne from the garden. I put it in a pot and strung it with fairy lights. It looked very magical indeed.

'We call it Corfu Christmas Tree,' Spiros Bear said. 'The leaves were chewed by the Pythia before she went into trance.'

What could be better, then, than a branch of a tree whose leaves were used by the oracle of Delphi? It was made for the job. It might cast a good spell.

We put strings of white lights in the end windows, the ones that could be seen from the road, and, just like at home, tried to keep them on the static setting. Every time there was a power cut, which was frequent, the lights would go back onto random, dazzling passers-by with a flashing sequence. It was just as well we did not live next to the sea. It could have been misinterpreted as an SOS: save me from the land of the lotus eaters.

'Your house, it look very nice,' Spiros Bear said. 'But why you have the lights flashing like that?'

I told him it was a tradition, wherever we lived. I couldn't let on that we were unable to master a simple light switch.

A few days before our 'at home', we found ourselves in AB, the supermarket that stocked Lye Cross Farm cheddar cheese from Somerset which was marketed by an acquaintance of mine and Burt's crisps, made by the son of someone who used to live in our village back in Dorset. We wanted a Westcountry twist to our event.

As Andreas spent ten minutes or so trying to decide which was the right flour, I wandered off only to return and find him in an animated conversation with a slim woman in her sixties, wearing bright red lipstick, a brocade jacket nipped in at the waist, tight ski pants and high-heeled jaguar print ankle boots.

'And this is my wife,' Andreas said, introducing the stranger as the granddaughter of Spiros, the factotum in *My Family and Other Animals*.

'I love the English,' she said, giving me a hug and then apologising for doing it.

'I cannot help touching,' she said, pinching my arm. 'Oops, there I go again.'

The Greeks are naturally gregarious. Andreas, with his bonhomie and warmth, fitted right in. I, meanwhile, had a tendency to sit on the sidelines and watch before getting too close. I knew it was part of people's exuberance; but hugging and kissing was never something that had ever come very naturally to me. It put me at a disadvantage with friends and with people from the Mediterranean. Meeting someone, even a friend, always put me in a slight state of anxiety as I never knew which side to kiss first. Invariably, I would go for the wrong side and end up clashing noses or glasses.

Afterwards, I thought about that encounter at the supermarket and concluded that of all the Greek gods in the pantheon, Andreas was Dionysus, the god of wine, joy, theatre and revelry. And me? Well, I was Hestia, the goddess of the hearth and home, who was so passive she gave up her Olympian seat to Dionysus to prevent heavenly conflict. We were chalk and cheese, but our stories were entwined irrevocably. And then I had another thought: I was thinking too much.

Back at the *kafenio*, Kiki – who was safely behind the counter so the kissing question never came into it – treated us to a cappuccino each and two honey and sesame seed bars.

'These are on me,' she said. 'The teachers say they are the best because they help you think.'

Think? That was probably not the best thing for me right now.

We told her she was very naughty.

'Always naughty.'

A whoosh of cold air flowed around our ankles as the door opened and a smartly dressed man in his sixties, with what my mother would call *a fine head of hair* and hawkish eyebrows, strutted in.

'This is the turkey man,' Kiki said.

Of course, Turkey Spiros.

So, using a mixture of Greek and English – *Gringlish* – we ordered a four-kilo turkey for our very first Christmas in Corfu.

It was the week before Christmas. Up in the *plateia*, the twin trees were strung with white fairy lights which had been switched on static, unlike our own. Set against the inky blue night sky, their twinkling brightness was magical. The kitchen smelt Christmassy. Andreas had been cooking for most of the day.

64

There were rillettes of pork in the oven and sliced oranges for Christmas decorations drying by the fire. And then the ants came in through the window and marched in single file across the oranges before going back out again for reinforcements.

After the oven had delivered some of its treats for our 'at home' in a few days' time, we strolled up to the *plateia* for a drink. Four glasses of wine later, Andreas took my hand (although it should have been the other way around, as I had drunk only two glasses) and we staggered home in the darkness. He had given me the impression that he had already prepared something for supper which would just need heating up. But it was now eight-thirty and he was planning to make a lasagne from scratch. After a self-imposed fast over the previous few days to get rid of my stomach upset, I was hungry enough to eat my own arm. It was a ridiculous argument, fuelled by drink.

I looked around the kitchen at all the debris from a day's cooking. Sunday's party had become all-consuming. He was obsessed with it.

'I want to go home,' I wailed as he checked his list of food for the party.

He didn't even bother to look up.

'Well, you sort your flights out and fuck off home then,' he said.

Shocked, I spent the night in the spare room, trying to keep warm under a thin summer duvet and thinking about what to do. I had wanted a reaction but I hadn't expected his.

The next morning, there was a reunion of sorts. He apologised, saying it was the drink that had been talking and that he was overwhelmed by all the catering he was having to do for Sunday. But that had been of his own choosing; and I said as much. So he retracted his apology and told me it was about time I did a bit more than mope all day. That was rich, given that I'd been cleaning, gardening and spending five hours a day writing fiction. There had still been no interest from *Saga*, the *Guardian* or *Myslexia* but I had managed to find a magazine here in Corfu which was publishing some of my articles. It wasn't much but it was a start. I was adding to the pot, albeit only a little, and I was feeling slightly more useful again.

After this outburst, I wanted to leave there and then. But I told him I would stay until May and then think about going home. I couldn't leave him to do all the decorating; it wouldn't have been fair. I also decided not to drink so much. The beakers of wine from the *kafenio* were lethal. I didn't want to be a stereotypical ex-pat drowning my sorrows in alcohol. Too much drink was a bad thing.

I thought about where I would stay when I got back. I couldn't live in my house because someone else was renting it. I was too old to move in with my elderly parents. And I couldn't impose myself on friends. Excuses, excuses.

I wasn't going to leave at all.

So I tried to block out all the hateful feelings that were eating me up and spitting me out. Live life, I told myself. And stop whining. It worked for a few days. But then it came back. It remained like that for weeks.

On the shortest day, it still didn't feel like Christmas in Corfu Town. There were a few lights on lampposts, but nothing to write home about. On a street corner, a choir of schoolgirls in Santa hats sang carols in Greek and the old town was full of young people who had broken up from school. Gangs of them roamed around, flirting and laughing. And the beggars were out in force, one prostrate, several with children and a few on crutches. There could be rich pickings at this time of year, even in a country where wealth wasn't exactly a national asset.

It is strange being in a foreign land at this time of year, especially when the native tongue is so hard to understand. I felt detached, I couldn't understand the overheard conversations going on around me. For one of life's eavesdroppers, I was lost. Any Christmas spirit in the air was going over my head. This surely had something to do with why I was finding it so hard to fit in. That and having left a very comfortable comfort zone behind in the UK. Even though he couldn't speak Greek, Andreas could talk about food and football. Every Corfiot is an expert in cooking and nearly all the men support football teams in the English premier division. My modus operandi is usually 'listen and observe'. My lack of Greek meant I could only do the latter.

Having called a temporary truce, we carried on cooking for our feast for Sunday. We had no idea how many people were coming and at what time, because Andreas could not remember if he had told them two o'clock or four. By the end of the Saturday, we had prepared most of the menu: sausage rolls, stuffed dates, red pepper hummus, red cabbage coleslaw, mince pies, Christmas cake, *kourambiedes* biscuits and *melamakarona* cakes, pavlova, crisps, nuts, cheese, coronation chicken, devils on horseback, salami and prosciutto on pumpernickel, smoked salmon and horseradish and melba toast and little tartlets filled with ratatouille.

Sunday dawned with a glorious burst of sunshine as we prepared our home for the party. House cleaned, food on the table, glad rags on, at one minute to two we were ready. At one minute past, the doorbell rang: Betty and Antonis and their three-year-old daughter, Marie Angela. Kisses planted on all cheeks. Doorbell rang again. Lambis. Kisses. Doorbell. Ilias, Koula and Little Ilias, aged six. A little later on, Gorgeous George and the serene Mrs George arrived, and then Yanni Pianni, flustered but here after a busy lunchtime in the taverna, and armed with a jar of preserved oranges made by his mother.. All the Greeks came bearing gifts: copious bottles of wine, a large azalea and a present we were allowed to open only at New Year. They didn't have much, these people, but we were discovered their generosity and hospitality was endless. There is a word in Greek – *philoxenia* – which means love, kindness and hospitality to foreigners, to strangers. That day, we grasped the concept of *philoxenia* first hand, by giving it and receiving it ourselves.

The children amused themselves with paper and crayons. Koula spoke Greek faster than anyone I know, her words sounding like rapid gunfire and all the time smiling her broad smile. I just nodded, hoping I was smiling in the right places. The men went outside to smoke and then came back in to teach Andreas how to play cards, dealing, as they always do in Greece, to the left. Master craftsman Lambis complimented me on my improvised Christmas tree – I could feel my head

67

inflating – and then took me to the dining room to show me a tiny ammonite hidden on the underside of one of the house's interior lintels. It was as if I was being shown a little bit of the Villa Oleander's soul.

The big man, Spiros Bear, was missing – off to the mainland on a family errand – which was probably just as well because he had an enormous appetite and there was only so much food to go around. They wolfed down my coronation chicken, made to a recipe from a retired chef back in our Dorset village for the Queen's Diamond Jubilee, as were all of Andreas' biscuits. And then, a few hours later, as quickly as they arrived, they went, one after another. The place was quiet now but there was an energy to the house I had not experienced before.

It had been a good day. The Christmas spirit had entered our home. And from that point on, I vowed to live in the moment, lucky indeed to be living the dream and experiencing the power of *philoxenia*.

Maybe my May departure would have to be reviewed.

On Christmas Eve, Andreas came back from the *kafenio* with a rather small plastic bag. He put it very carefully on the kitchen worktop. Dean Martin sang 'Let it Snow' in the background.

'What's that?' I asked, thinking he'd probably picked up some garlic from the mini-market.

'It's the turkey.'

Turkey? The creature inside the bag was the smallest thing I'd ever seen. A swallow would have had more meat on it. If there was such a thing as the runt of the flock, then we'd got it. It was the turkey at the back, the one that came last when the birds scurried across the village road to avoid a passing scooter rider. It was the cougher, the wheezer, pigeon rather than barrel chested. If it could have spoken it would have had a high-pitched voice like the comedian Joe Pasquale.

'Well, we'll just have to supplement it with plenty of potatoes,' I said, as I pulled a bowl of Delia's chestnut and apple stuffing on to the worktop next to it. Stuffing it was difficult. It still had all its entrails inside. And attached. After a hairy few minutes wrestling with the innards of the world's smallest turkey, Andreas passed the bird to me for stuffing. There was a problem. I could barely get my hand inside. Once I did, I opened it out to spread the stuffing around, closed my hand to take it out, but my knuckles got stuck. The whole she-bang was in danger of turning into a Mr Bean sketch. I closed my eyes and willed my hand smaller. It was no good, I was going to have a dead turkey on my right hand for the whole of the festive period. It wasn't as if I could cover it up with a glove. I'd have to tuck it inside a sling or something. But by the time we got to Boxing Day, surely it would be starting to smell? All these thoughts raced through my head as Andreas picked up a bottle of olive oil on the counter.

'Try this,' he said, dribbling the oil down my wrist.

I have often heard about the magical properties of olive oil. And it lived up to its reputation. Within seconds, there was enough lubrication to oil the internal workings of a steam engine. With one hand on the turkey and another on the kitchen drawer, Andreas pulled and tugged and pulled until, with an enormous squelch, the turkey broke free and flew across the kitchen. More important than the turkey's great escape was that my hand was now free and none the worse for its ordeal. After a giggling fit that lasted at least five minutes, we scooped the turkey up from the floor, washed it, patted it dry with kitchen roll and stuffed it with a spoon, trussed it up and put it into a baking tray.

'Let's get this little bleeder into the oven and have done with it,' Andreas said. So on Christmas Eve, we sat down, just the two of us, to a turkey the size of a thimble (it seemed to have shrunk during the cooking process) and all the trimmings, preceded by giant prawns from the market and smoked salmon. With makeshift paper hats as we had been unable to find Christmas crackers in the shops, we wished each other happy Christmas when midnight arrived, Skyped the children, and then sat down to watch the final episode of our boxed set of *24* before we exchanged presents.

On Christmas morning, the church bells clanged at just after seven-thirty and then again at nine.

A little old man with a wizened face and a young man with an enormous moustache were outside ringing the bells of the tower next to the church. The younger man was joined by his son, who took hold of the rope and went up with it, several times, before being rescued by his father. We followed two smartly dressed people from the *plateia* in through the north door, eager to see how the Greek Orthodox church celebrated Christmas Day. The service had already been going for at least an hour. The church was full: men at the front, singing responses to the litany as the white-and-gold-robed priest stood the other side of the iconostasis. We could see the priest through the central door as he faced the holy table, like a conjuror, with his back to the audience, performing magic. The surroundings and chanting were spiritual but, at the same time, the comings and goings of the congregation seemed very informal. Two small children ran up and down the aisle: a boy with gelled hair and a girl with a new Barbie doll. A woman put a euro in the box at the front, pulled out a candle and lit it. The air conditioning units blasted out hot air as the faces we'd seen gazing down at cards in the *kafenio* said their prayers. There was the man we called Spiros Ron who looked like an older and smaller version of Andreas's brother. He was wearing a smart black coat, neatly pressed, light grey trousers and black, highly polished loafers. And there was the teacher of ancient Greek, who was normally so vociferous when he was losing at cards. In here he was as meek as a lamb.

This was the first time I had been inside this church, which was one of six in the village. It was the community's main place of worship and the ceilings and walls were adorned with wonderfully over-the-top paintings of saints sitting on clouds, a big, bearded, terrifying God pontificating, Adam and Eve expelled from Eden and a delicious devil on judgment day. In the corner of one picture I could see God taking a rest from creating the world by sitting down next to a unicorn. Above our heads were huge, glinting chandeliers, weighed down by a hundred light-bulbs. The fact that we understood none of the language of the service added to the mystery. A mobile phone rang just as the three male voices at the front achieved harmony. The collection was taken, the congregation collectively crossed itself and then there was a power cut. The lights went out, including the overhead 'candles', which were electric fakes, and the wooden seats suddenly became very cold. The church's garish interior was lit only by the candles in memory of loved ones, shafts of sunlight piercing through two small stained glass windows and a laser beam of sunshine shooting through the south door.

The electricity came back on, signalled by a melodic ping-ping-ping from the air conditioning units, and the priest distributed the holy bread. Outside, the women chattered as the men went into the *kafenio* for coffee and a game of cards. Turkey Spiros shouted in Greek from the corner that our two coffees had been taken care of. We put our thumbs up and told him our Christmas turkey had been excellent. And then Kiki, who, like a modern-day Athena, dispensed wisdom along with drinks from behind the counter, gave me a pomegranate for New Year's Day to break on the ground for luck.

'Take this,' she said. 'It will be good for your year ahead.'

Down on the beach at Paleokastritsa, I sat on the wall as Andreas went in for a Christmas Day swim. We were the only ones on a beach which in summer would be packed. It made a change from the usual rainy or overcast festive season back home.

Up at Dukas for pork in the oven, Spiros Waiter hovered around Andreas and then remarked on Andreas's aftershave.

'Georgio Armani?' he said. 'Next time you go in England, you get me some? Or some Timberland boots? I give you money.'

'Of course,' the ever-obliging Andreas said. And I bet I'd have to give up some of my hand luggage allowance to accommodate Spiros Waiter's latest whim.

After a leisurely lunch, made all the more leisurely because neither of us had to cook it, it was off towards Corfu Town to our friends Gorgeous George and his wife for Christmas evening drinks. The Graceful Mrs G was the type who would look serene in a sack. I ought to have hated her for it, but she is divine.

Sitting in the splendour of their *Dynasty*-style house with its three hundred and sixty degree view of the island, Mrs George turned to me and told me about their great Christmas Day disappointment. She had been persuaded by George to put on a chiffon ball gown with sparkling diamanté jewellery. On their own at Christmas for the first time ever, they had dressed for dinner, just the two of them, and sat down at their large table like the lord and lady from their favourite television programme.

'You know,' said Gorgeous George. 'The English one. *Downton Abbey*.'

He pronounced it Down-tonne.

As the serene Mrs George beamed like a graceful swan, Gorgeous George, resplendent in dinner jacket and bow tie, had lifted the domed lid from the silver platter, to reveal a turkey which, to their dismay, was not much bigger than a sparrow.

'It was very small,' Mrs George said. 'There was no meat on the breast. We had to have extra vegetables.'

It was something we could picture very well and we chuckled as we drove back to the village to watch last year's *Downton Abbey* Christmas special. I had never watched this programme at all in England. But over here, with Greek television channels full of black and white films, shouty political debates and endless showing of the same, badly-shot pictures on the news, I had become a fan of anything in English. I was now intimately acquainted with *Upstairs Downstairs*, *Downton*, *The Closer* and *NCIS*. I needed to get a life.

Boxing Day was as dead as a dodo. Normally so manic at home in the UK, with thirty or more crammed into my parents' cottage. Andreas spent the day listening to football. I sighed deeply and loudly but he had his earphones in and couldn't hear me. I went for a walk around the olive groves instead.

In the days after Christmas, we took the car out and went north. Our first stop was Kassiopi, a small resort in the north west, with the ruins of a Byzantine castle and pretty harbour. We had stayed here several times in the past and it was an ideal place to come on holiday with children. It's one of those places which has cashed in on the tourism boom of previous years but still retains plenty of character. The village is at the top edge of the area known as Kensington-on-Sea (because of all the posh villas dotted on the hillsides overlooking the Corfu Channel) but it's a popular a holiday destination among people of all classes and wealth, with plenty of tavernas, bars, apartments to rent, buckets and spades and postcards on sale, alongside shops with little old ladies sitting outside making lace to sell. One of Kassiopi's most famous visitors is said to have been the decadent Roman Emperor Nero. These days, you are likely to find Italians and Brits staying here, with the odd luxury yacht calling in before setting off down the coast for lunch at Agni or for a pre-arranged dinner date with the Rothschild family on their walled and turreted estate.

The highest point on the island is Mount Pantokrator, which is often covered in mist. From this spot you get a real sense of the island's geography and how it sits in relation to the mainland. But it was at the wonderful Angelokastro, a Byzantine bastion north of Paleokastritsa, that I felt revitalised. There is a long, steep climb to the top and the feeling of being in touch with the past here is very strong. Was that pirates or Venetians I saw as I looked out to sea towards the Diapontia islands? They disappeared into the white horses of surf as I turned inland to see the tops of mountains and across to Corfu Town. And, by my feet, empty graves carved out of the rock.

'This is good, isn't it?' Andreas said, grasping my arm.

Indeed it was. And there on the windswept outcrop, this inhospitable place that had served the defence of the island so well, we hugged. As Kiki would say, we were okay, at least until the next fall-out.

Down then to the village of Lakones and its fabulous view out across the five emerald bays of Paleokastritsa. It's one of the best vistas on the island. The beauty of this resort is best admired from above, as the rocks and olives and cypresses tumble into the sea. We travelled on and down, around switchback bends to meet the main road to get back home.

In the *kafenio*, the noisy card games went on night after night, punctuated by the odd game of football on the television and the National Geographic channel. Alekos and Nikos, the noisiest card players in the world, raised their voices in a loud, angry gabble as they slapped their cards down with vigour. They were the two most educated men in the *kafenio* but in here they were equal; so they had to assert their superiority by demonstrating who could shout the loudest. On the National

Geographic channel, the old men liked best the scenes of mating animals and ones showing predators chasing their prey.

'Look,' said Spiros Waiter, pointing to the television. 'Crocodile.'

He gave his Mutley hiss and showed his teeth.

And then he pointed to his feet and said: 'Don't forget the Timberland boots. Size forty-one.'

On our first New Year's Eve away from home, on our Big Fat Grown-up Greek Gap Year in Corfu, we had planned to celebrate in our *plateia*, with its pretty white lights strung on the trees, which so reminded us of our village square back home. In Dorset, the party would be going full swing, with our neighbours hosting a wondrous feast for twelve of our friends. After fine dining in their best bib and tucker (it's what we would have hosted, had we been there) they would probably head into the pub across the square for more drinks. After fighting their way through a six-deep queue to get a drink, there would be a shout of 'It's five to twelve!' and a stampede would head out of the door for the midnight celebrations.

An orderly circle would form in the middle of the road, oblivious to any vehicle that attempted to get through. There would be two choruses of 'Auld Lang Syne' and then, if you were lucky, the church clock would strike thirteen. Party poppers would be launched, there would be kisses all round from people you hadn't spoken to all year, you'd declare undying love for the village and all its inhabitants and proclaim you wouldn't want to be anywhere else.

This is the memory I had of New Year's Eve in our Dorset village. So when the Christmas tree lights went on in our Greek village on the same day that the Dorset festive decorations were officially launched, we naturally thought our Christmas and New Year celebrations would follow suit. The same but different. In a Greek way. We had already discovered Christmas in Greece was quite different. Surely New Year would seem more familiar?

So we went to the *kafenio* for a coffee to check what time they closed. 'Ten o'clock,' Kiki's brother, the taciturn baker Thassos, said.

It was clear the village would not be celebrating New Year's Eve like its Dorset counterpart. However, New Year, we were told, was bigger than Christmas in Greece (although not as big as Easter which is huge). It's when St Vassilis takes presents to the children after they have gone around the village wearing Santa hats and carrying triangles in a determined effort to knock on as many doors as they can, sing a few bars of an obscure Greek carol and expect to be paid for it. So, surely, New Year's Eve, which is celebrated the world over with fireworks, fountains and fanfares, would be pretty special.

Maybe Corfu Town, that lively, stylish capital, would be where it was all happening. By eleven o'clock, the bars were beginning to close. The bag lady who sat outside Marks and Spencer day and night, with a big hooded parka and sunglasses several sizes too big for her, was in her usual place. A bearded man sat under a colonnade near the Church of St Spyridon and the town eccentric sat with a Santa hat on in a fold-up chair outside the newsagents, his big fat lips talking Greek gibberish to no-one in particular. In the Bristol bar, a surly waiter more concerned with his quiff than his customer service – surprising considering there were only three customers including the two of us – gave me the weakest *cuba libre* I have ever encountered, with enough ice to fill Alaska.

So at eleven thirty we headed home. Maybe the *kafenio* was open. But in the square, the lights were out, with just three people playing cards in one of the tavernas. It was five to midnight.

We drove back home, quickly lit the fire and popped open a cork. I put on Zorba's Dance and turned up the volume, just as we rang our dinner party friends back home.

'Is that Charlie?' I said, when our old neighbour from Dorset answered the phone.

'Yes, who's that?'

So easily forgotten.

And then, it seems, we were being passed around the Dorset dinner table.

'What are you up to then?' someone asked Andreas.

'Oh, we've got a house full of people. There's Spiros, Spiros and Ilias…um…Koula, Marianna, Natalia, Spiros and someone

75

whose name I can't remember…another Spiros…and Maddie's dancing with Lambis. Hang on, I'll just go and get her.'

After a reasonable delay, I put the phone to my ear and pretended to be out of breath.

'I'm impressed,' our English neighbour said. 'I hope you'll be bringing back some of these Greek New Year's Eve traditions.'

'Um, maybe,' I said. 'Sorry, I must go: Lambis is just teaching me a new dance step and Andreas is getting the plates ready for smashing.'

It was all nonsense of course. They don't even smash plates in Corfu and, if they do, it's only for the tourists.

'I'm so pleased you're having a lovely time,' our neighbour said. 'We're having a ball.'

In the Dorset background I could hear laughter and three champagne corks popping one after the other. So I got Andreas to ring our doorbell, open and slam it and shout *kalispera* five times in five different voices.

We said goodbye to our English friends, with Andreas doing background noises in the best drunken Greek-guest-style he could manage, and then we put the phone down.

I turned down the music and the two of us gazed into the fire.

'Well, that's the quietest New Year's Eve I think I've ever had,' he said, as I texted everyone who had ever given me their mobile phone number. 'Shall we go to bed?'

January

The wine dark juice of pomegranate stained the paving slabs, the seeds spilling out like the innards of road-kill. It is a Greek tradition on New Year's Day to smash a pomegranate on the ground for luck. Its seeds are symbolic of fertility and the act is a blessing for the year to come while Persephone still sleeps with Hades in the dark underworld during the winter. When she emerges, it will be spring, the light will change and the ground and air will become warmer. But until then, she is destined to stay with the underworld king. Only the pleading of her mother, Demeter, allows her to resurface after winter has passed. Had Demeter not struck this deal with Hades, it would have been forever winter, with Demeter, the goddess of the harvest, withdrawing her labour in protest.

It was eight o'clock on New Year's Day and the sun was straining to clamber in through the French windows. I got up and let it in.

A ginger cat was curled up on a cushion on the terrace outside, having successfully defended its territory in an horrendous bust-up with one of the many other village cats about an hour before. It was triumphant in round one and had gone back to bed.

Up on the hillside, an occasional gunshot broke the silence and then ricocheted around the valley. This set off a chain of barking dogs which, in turn, launched the geese into their daily honking in the garden next door. And then the cockerels began their alarm call of cock-a-doodle-dooing from here to the next village and down to the sea. A thrush warbled, a robin broke out into verses and then the church bells clang-clang-clanged for the second round of the church service to celebrate St Vassilis' Day.

In previous years, we would have been nursing a hangover the size of a small town as we woke up on the morning after the night before. But not this time. Although not for the want of trying.

77

It was the name day of the lovely Kiki from the *kafenio* so today the cakes were on her. It was said that if you had a slice of St Vassilis' cake and bit into a coin, you would have luck all year, although you might have needed a trip to the dentist.

We went back to Mount Pantokrator, named after The Almighty, but yet again, the top of it – at 2,972 feet the highest point on Corfu – was concealed by mist, obscuring the sides of the road where it drops to oblivion. On a clear day, you can see Italy from this mountain, even though it's eighty miles away. It is the perfect spot to see the whole of the island laid out before you, and Albania just across the channel. It's a good place to get your bearings, to find your place, where you fit in. But I couldn't see anything.

In the days around Christmas and New Year, gangs of children in Santa hats roamed the streets and lanes of towns and villages. On our doorstep, a young boy carried a triangle and clanged it tunelessly as he and his friends sang a seasonal song.

'*Kali Xronia*!' they said in unison.

'I think they want money,' I said to Andreas, who produced from his wallet five euros which were grabbed by the biggest child who then promptly ran away.

Five minutes later, there was another batch, and then another, and then another.

'Maybe that was too much,' I said. 'They've obviously gone round the corner and told their friends.'

At the *kafenio*, Kiki laughed.

'You just give them a few cents or sweets,' she said, warning us that at the rate we were giving, we'd have the whole village around our front door. 'For five euros, *I* play triangle and sing to you.'

It was a joke but with a serious undertone. Despite their joviality and love of life, these people did not have much. There were long faces in the *kafenio* every time the news came on. And in Corfu Town where I handed over the princely sum of three euros to the cobbler who had stuck the soles back on my boots, he handed me a receipt and said: 'The receipt is for me and the money is for Merkel.'

On 6 January the shadows were long. It was chilly out of the sun. The men wore bobble hats to fight off the cold air while the women found thicker headscarves to keep their ears warm. The daphne trees blew wildly and clouds scudded across the top of the mountain. In the *plateia*, the church bells rang for Epiphany. The women came bearing Mythos glasses, ceramic jugs in the shape of sweetcorn or chickens, and bottles that once contained Grolsch beer or ouzo – any receptacle they could lay their hands on in which to receive the holy water blessed by the priest.

The area in front of the iconostasis was decorated with arches of palm from our trees, interspersed with pretty coloured lights, which reflected the highly coloured paintings. In the centre arch, someone had fastened an incongruous flashing circle, which looked rather like a wheel of fortune. The body of the church was packed with people. Men, women and children came and went. A small girl sat on the chancel rail and hugged her moustachioed father's legs when it was his turn to chant the litany. From behind the screen on the iconostasis, the priest's voice boomed, projecting his power and closeness to the divine for all to hear. Every time the priest emerged from the door, the congregation got up, a never ending see-saw of those devoted and those who had trouble standing for long periods. By 10.30am the priest had recited a long passage and there was yawning, fidgeting, scratching and quiet talking at the back. The seats were hard and the cold came up through the stone floor into my feet, despite thick tights and shoes. The wheel of fortune kept on flashing at the front; there was a smell of incense in the air, and its smoke curled through the shafts of light coming in high through the windows. Little children balanced on one leg up the central aisle and there were sharp 'shushes' as their chatter became too loud. The *kafenio* crowd had surged to the front while the wives and daughters worried about the lamb cooking at home. Was the oven on at the right temperature? A boy did kung fu moves in the aisle. A mobile phone went off, its ring tone a theme tune from a Greek soap opera. The woman owner answered it and had a conversation. There was loud chanting at the front, everyone got up and the bells rang outside.

We funnelled down to the front to collect the blessed bread, as we had done before Christmas. The priest was at the door, with a cross in one hand and a bunch of rosemary and jonquils in the other. He flicked everyone – apart from us – with water and wished them *xronia polla*.

I came away from the church with mixed feelings. I had wanted to witness the Greeks at worship on this special day of Epiphany. I wanted to experience it and respect it; but the priest had not been friendly, probably because it was obvious we weren't orthodox or had done something wrong. It was clearly a misunderstanding. But Andreas had other ideas. In the *kafenio*, he mulled it over and then went back to talk to the priest. He told me afterwards that the conversation went something like this:

'Why did you bless everyone else with the holy water and not us?'

We knew that only one person in the village had been confirmed, so it could not have been that.

'Your wife, she took the bread,' the priest hissed. 'And she did not kiss the icon.'

'We did not know,' Andreas said. 'In my church, the priest would have welcomed you, whatever your religion.'

As a parting shot, the priest offered Andreas some holy water.

'It is blessed for one hundred years; you take.' It sounded like an olive branch.

Back in the *kafenio*, the incident had opened up something.

'I made a mistake,' I said to Andreas, embarrassed. 'Please don't make a fuss about it. I shouldn't have been in the church anyway.'

It was true. It was hypocritical when I didn't believe in god or religion. But I had wanted to get a feel for this way of life which meant so much to the village people. The church was always so crowded, with people of all ages, not just old folk. Back home, the best our church could rustle up on a good day might be a few dozen. And maybe, somewhere, deep down, I was hoping for a sign, a spiritual experience that might set me on the road to redemption.

One of the men in the *kafenio* interjected.

80

'It is okay. It is same for me. The priest will not bless my house,' he said. 'Because I am not married and live with girl.'

'The priest is not happy how the people are in this village. How they play cards and go in and out of the church as if they don't seem to care,' said another.

'His face, it is not happy,' said yet another.

'He not like women,' said another.

Suddenly, my predicament had opened up the hearts of the *kafenio* community, who offered me a glass of *tsipouro*, ouzo, coffee or whatever I wanted. Kiki's father, Michalis, made me a frothy cappuccino.

It was heartwarming, both the coffee and the reaction my encounter had provoked, although I did feel rather foolish. I had obviously done something wrong but it was out of ignorance rather than disrespect. Religious rituals fascinate me but, today, my Epiphany moment was the revelation of the kindness of human nature. As far as organised worship was concerned, I could admire the lights, the smells, the sights, the spirituality, even if I didn't believe. From here on in, I vowed I would still go to church services every now and then but stay, observing, from the back. That was a more honest position.

Across the *plateia* in the *kafenio*, the men were in playful mood as they gathered like gunslingers in a Western saloon bar. They grabbed their cards from the counter, collected pens and paper, and got into position as the National Geographic Channel showed the latest programme about predators and their prey.

Outside, the fish man arrived in his red van, announcing himself with a plaintive *psaria* over a loudspeaker. The assembled crowd went out to have a look at his catch, like they did every other night, and went back in again without buying anything. Hardly any of them ever bought a drink and none of them appeared to feel guilty about using the *kafenio* facilities and then complaining about the prices in the mini-market.

A scooter held together by bits of string rattled its way up into the *plateia*, its distinctive one-gear sound filling the evening air. Its rider, a fifty-something man with a shaved head and Mohican strip and white sunglasses perched above his eyes, dismounted. He was wearing long bell-bottomed jeans and a short-sleeved muscle top.

He introduced himself as Yannis.

'My mother is Elizabeth from the taverna,' he said. 'My daughter, she work there now, with her mother. You like a drink?'

So we sat with Yannis at the bar of the *kafenio* as he swore and blasphemed his way around the best spots of the island he thought we should visit.

'Believe me, you see, it will be big surprise for you,' he said. 'I go to Angelokastro on my bike and the weather, it was bad, you know? And then I was blown off my facking bike by the— what you say…?'

'Weeend,' says Spiros Waiter looking up from his cards. All this time he had been listening to the conversation and we hadn't even realised he was there. 'Forty-one,' he added, in yet another reference to the boots he had asked us to bring back the next time we visited England

The conversation brought others out of the woodwork. It appeared after our run-in with the priest, we were true locals.

Rather like the scene from *One Flew Over The Cuckoo's Nest* in which the Native American speaks for the first time – his words being 'Um, juicy fruit' on being offered a chewing gum – a man we had seen regularly for the last three months suddenly piped up.

'So you from England, yes?' In his late sixties and with bushy eyebrows, he had been here every night we had been in. He had reminded me of one of my son's friends so in my head he was known as Greek Dave. His accent was distinctly American.

'I live in Canada for twenty-three years,' he said, introducing himself as George. From that point onwards, we referred to him as Canadian George. He was to become one of our favourites.

Outside, the white lights twinkled in the trees, a stray dog howled along a street of squashed lemons and pomegranate and a wobbly scooter rider made his way home after one glass of *tsipouro* too many. It felt like home.

We were due to leave Corfu again for another visit to England, this time to be there for my daughter who was due to have her third child by C-section. Just before we were about to go, Kiki pressed a large parcel in my hand. For her name day on 1 January, I had given her a copy of *The Cat of Portovecchio*, a novel about Corfu in the 1950s written by someone I knew in Dorset.

'This is for you,' she said. 'It is the best.'

I opened the wrapping paper and pulled out a huge coffee table book, *Corfu: The Garden Isle*, containing beautiful pictures and essays about the island.

It was far too generous. But I couldn't refuse, it would have been impolite. How could I ever thank her? And then I realised, a thank you or *efharisto* was adequate. There was no more to say.

The storm threatened to turn our solidly-built house completely inside out. I was huddled up so tightly, I expected at any minute to see the jacaranda tree walk hand-in-hand through the front door with the oleander in a kind of Arthur-Rackham-meets-Edward-Lear-type moment.

'Give us shelter,' they would have pleaded.

Rain poured through the end windows, *drip-plop-torrent*. The wind roared and whistled down the chimney in such a terrifying way that, for a split second, I turned to see the shadow of Andreas and thought it was the convict Abel Magwitch from *Great Expectations*. I shuddered.

And then the thunder cracked, splitting the sky in two after a great flash of light like an Olympian paparazzi ready to pounce on the world's greatest scoop. The previous day, it had rained and rained and rained and then there was a tiny bit of sunshine. Almost enough blue to make a sailor a pair of trousers, albeit a very small one. But even a midget matelot would have done for me. After the trauma of my daughter's last pregnancy, we had volunteered to go home to do school runs and other duties, at least for ten days. With hindsight, maybe going home again so soon was not doing my homesickness any favours. But my family needed me. And, more to the point, I needed them.

Direct flights to Gatwick didn't start until the end of April. We checked our bags in and waited for our plane to Athens, after being dropped off by Spiros Bear, hair freshly washed and flicked. But our plane never arrived. The visibility over Corfu was so poor, the flight was cancelled at the eleventh hour. We would miss our connection at Athens. So we made new plans and set off the following day. The sense of anticipation was well and truly mounting. We were just two days away from the C-section. Would we make it? Especially with the UK gripped in a snowstorm. It was at times like this that it dawned on me just how far I was from home. Over a thousand miles, beyond the tip of Italy, on the same latitude as Uzbekistan, China and Tennessee.

On Facebook, a big argument was raging amongst ex-pats now living in Corfu about the pros and cons of Kavos. Was its reputation, and its appeal to the Channel 4 documentary makers, damaging to the rest of the island? Or was it just a place for the young to let off steam? From the television, we learnt that there was a big debate in Parliament about wealthy Greeks with friends in high places who had evaded tax, and demands for them to be accountable like the rest of the population. On my phone there was a text from my daughter:

> Hope you'll soon be here Mum.
> Need you.

In the *kafenio*, the card games and the shouting continued.

'You not gone yet?' said Canadian George. We explained our predicament and then Spiros Waiter walked in. He picked up two packs of cards from the counter and some scraps of paper which had been election fliers in a previous life to write down the scores.

'You are still here, Margarita?' he said, eyebrows raised.

We explained again.

'You go to Athens, you visit my restaurant,' he said. He wrote its name down, along with his own, on a piece of paper.

'You must visit it,' he said. And then he leaned over the table to Andreas and said: 'Don't forget the shoes.'

Spiros Waiter was a man obsessed with labels. Labels and football. Those were his passions.

The next day, the planes from Corfu were flying; so we set off to Athens where we had an overnight stop. By then, I was so concerned about missing the flight home that I insisted we stayed close to the airport. It was a comfortable but overpriced chain hotel. We had plenty of time so we took the bus into town. We were heading for Monastiraki Square, armed with Spiros Waiter's piece of paper.

'When you go in Athens,' he had said, 'you take this.'

It was dark by the time the bus dropped us off in Syntagma Square, not far from the Greek Parliament. This spot is a social hub and transport hub; everything stops at Syntagma. From 2010 to 2012, the square was the site of mass protests, including an occupation, against the economic crisis. Depending on who was reporting the figures, between 10,000 and 50,000 demonstrated here. The occupiers have now been removed and demonstrations are less frequent although the people are still angry. We walked through Athens' busy streets, parts of which had been pedestrianised since our last visit a few years ago. Despite poverty and violence, the city felt no different from when we had visited some years before the crisis. It lived and breathed as normal, although I couldn't help imagining an undercurrent going on behind the façade of men and women walking past department store windows and smiling as if they were strolling in Exeter, Reading or Manchester.

An old man latched on to us and asked us where we were from and where we were going. We showed him our bit of paper.

'I take you to better taverna,' he said, obviously on commission every time he introduced a new customer. 'The place you looking for is like McDonald's of Athens. The place I show you is much better.'

We followed him for part of the way and then our paths separated. We explained we were on a mission for a friend and the old man just smiled and wished us goodnight.

Down in Monastiraki, we held our piece of paper up to see if it matched any of the signs and then asked a man in a kiosk for directions. It was right behind us. We had only eaten out in Athens once before and – bizarrely - this was the same place. Bouzouki music filled the few gaps there were in *Sigalas-Bairaktaris*, a very popular fast food taverna where the only problem was finding a place to sit. The noise of customers chatting was deafening and the waiters and waitresses had probably been Olympic runners in a previous life, so quick were they on their feet. We were shown a table for two, ordered a plate of meat and salad and looked around. The walls were covered in framed photographs of the proprietor and famous people who had eaten at the taverna.

When our *gyros pita* arrived, we passed our piece of paper to the waiter. He looked at us, puzzled.

'This is from Spiros Papas?'

'Yes, he is our friend.'

And then a broad grin went across the waiter's face. He turned to another waiter and showed him the paper. The other waiter laughed and then showed another. There was laughter all around.

'He is all right?'

'Yes, he's fine, he just wanted us to say hello.'

They laughed again.

'He is crazy,' our waiter said. 'Here, have a karafe of wine on the house.'

From that moment onwards, we were treated like royalty. All the note had said was that he, Spiros Waiter, was our friend and they should treat us well. It was a modern-day example of *tesserae hospitalis*, the tokens of mutual hospitality in Magna Grecia that were exchanged between parties and then passed on by fathers to their sons as evidence of their entitlement. In ancient times, if you moved around a lot, your earthenware *tessera hospitalis* was a lifeline. If you were in a strange town and claimed hospitality from someone your ancestor knew many years ago, you would be asked to produce your *tessera* for inspection. If it was genuine, you could expect to be treated like old friends. And so it was in *Sigalas-Bairaktaris*.

'It is okay,' the proprietor said, when we went to pay. 'This meal is on us. Say hello to Spiros when you return.'

Back in England and the country was frozen to a standstill. We arrived just in time to welcome baby girl Number Three to the world, do the school run for Number One and then engage in battle with Number Two, whose favourite word was *no*, said very loudly. It was a typical English winter. We got stuck in snow in the dark on the main road at the aptly-named Three Sisters, west of Dorchester, as we headed back after a hospital visit. And then, a few days later, we battled flood water and faced three diversions in the space of thirty minutes to travel a few miles. An old friend with whom we were staying called me the wrong name every time he looked at me. How quickly I'd been forgotten. We'd only been away for four months. But it seemed like a lifetime.

Back in Dorset, the soggy, syrupy mist swooped down all of a sudden and I wanted to grab hold of it. It was my security blanket, wrapped around me, as I gazed at water droplets on sodden and bare trees and rotten cider apples lying on the ground. I loved this place. I said goodbye to my family and, as we packed up and got ready to go back to Corfu, I looked out of the window where the sunlight bounced off the bantams' backs. Even in winter, when my Dorset village was up to her neck in fog, the theme music to *A Summer Place* was always playing in my head.

My friend asked who I missed the most. I had to think. Family, friends were fundamental things which I had come to realise should never be taken for granted. But, no, it wasn't a single person. It was the place itself. For the first three months of living in Corfu, guilt had picked me up and dropped me down again as I fought the urge to go home. Who wouldn't be happy in this lovely place, this lovely island of Corfu, with its beautiful, kind people and wonderful scenery? What gave me the right to feel like this? How pathetic was I, when most people would give their right arm to be in my situation? I felt especially guilty for feeling like this at a time when so many Greeks were going through such hardship.

'It's just the way you feel,' my friend said, like a wise and patient Penelope. 'Guilt is the most destructive thing. Don't feel bad about feeling bad. Just accept it and then enjoy what you're doing and what you've got.'

I knew she was right. It would have been the same advice I would have given anyone else. Seize the day! After two weeks away and a tedious journey home – each of us carrying one of SW's new boots in our hand luggage – I woke up in my Greek bed with a knot in my stomach, thinking about my dear new granddaughter and her sisters. I thought about my old dad in Somerset, sitting in his chair next to the Rayburn; and about my mother, bustling about as twelve inches of snow melted outside. I thought about my Dorset village friends around a dinner table enjoying good food, wine and company. I thought about singing 'Drink Up Thy Zider' as the Bristol City fans danced at a 2-1 win over Ipswich the previous Saturday. And I didn't even *like* football.

And then I looked out of the window onto my Corfu village. The sun was shining over the mountain and the mimosa had burst out into brilliant yellow droplets almost overnight.

Life was not so bad.

February

'Are you coming up to St Simeon tomorrow?' asked Canadian George at the *kafenio* on Saturday night.

We were planning to, if we could get out of bed that early the next morning.

'You know about the place and why it is there, don't you?' he said, pulling up a seat as the card players and television presenters yelled in the background.

We leaned forward to hear him better.

'The grandparents of Ilias's wife, Koula, they were digging up there, farming, you know, and they found a picture of the saint.'

We leaned even further forward, our chairs in danger of going over the tipping point. This was gripping stuff.

'Well,' George said, tugging on the peak of his baseball cap, 'they took it home, you know, brushed it off and put it in a frame on the wall.'

He wiggled around in his chair, anticipating the punchline.

'The next day, they come downstairs and the picture, it is gone. They go back up the mountain and there the picture is, you know, back in the ground where they found it. So they built the church there for Saint Simeon.'

It was an incredible story and we were hooked. The next morning, we made the long trek up a goat path and then a donkey track in our Sunday best, apart from our shoes because we decided hiking boots and trainers were probably better than high heels. The tiny church sat on a terrifying pinnacle of rock jutting out of the mountains on the road to Paleokastritsa. It belonged to Koula, the sister of Spiros Bear, and was used only on its name day and for the occasional wedding.

From eight o'clock on 3 February, St Simeon's Day, people began to arrive in dribs and drabs, in cars and on foot and in a minibus with two pick-ups from the *plateia*. It was a windy

89

morning and the red ribbons attached to a bell hung from a metal pole in the ground flew out like the tails of a kite.

They walked down the rocky path, with its well-worn steps carved out of the earth and boulders, edges newly-painted white. The little church clung to its rock like a limpet mine on a ship's hull. There was a sense of danger up there in the clouds. Any moment we could have toppled right over the edge. Nausea overwhelmed me as we peeped out over the sheer drop to the valley floor below. In the distance we could see Paleokastritsa harbour, the monastery and the wine-dark sea. To the south the village of Liapades, marching up the hill, and to the left the fertile plains of the Ropa Valley, with its gypsies and market gardens. Out across the olives and cypress trees there was Corfu Town, the old fort, the islands of Lazaretto and Vidos sitting in the water and, across the channel, the snow-capped mountains of the mainland and Albania. We craned our necks around to see the road along the mountains and villages falling from the sky and tumbling down the hillside. It was a terrifying, heart-in-the-mouth feeling of vertigo. Not a place to bring a small child. You might just as well have left a baby to chance in the middle of a busy road. By nine o'clock there was a steady stream of people, carrying plastic bags which they placed at the top of the path. In each one there was a bottle of wine, ready for celebrations later.

Outside the little church, which had been whitewashed especially for the occasion, a crowd of people wearing woolly hats and thick coats were talking, smoking and laughing. Ilias and his sons Antonis and Simos gave us a wave. And then we saw Spiros Ron, Theodoros Matt Monro and others from the *kafenio*. As we drew closer, Turkey Spiros, Canadian George and Paleo Spiros popped up from behind a large boulder.

'Would you like a drink?' Canadian George said.

I frowned in surprise. A drink?

'This is a celebration, you know, a village tradition,' he said. I look towards the church.

'You won't be able to get in,' he said. 'Too busy.'

Ilias brought out a bottle of whisky from the inside pocket of his leather coat and Turkey Spiros proffered a bottle of *tsipouro*. The weathered holes in the rock made perfect holders for six plastic cups.

And still they came down the path. There was a low, loud voice and I looked up to see Spiros Bear in a bright yellow Puffa jacket coming down to join the throng.

'Didn't expect to see you here at church,' I said.

'Him is tradition,' he said.

The edges of the precipice had been painted white, just in case anyone was thinking of peering over the sheer drop.

With minutes to go until the end of the service at ten-thirty, still they came. They lit candles in memory of loved ones and placed them in a rickety, green box looked after by the little old man in a bomber jacket. Meanwhile, Turkey Spiros and Canadian George poured a never-ending stream of liquor into the plastic cups.

Ilias emerged from the church carrying a breadbasket with a blue bag inside it. Euro notes were put into it by the assembled throng, which by now numbered fifty or sixty. Collection. Beyond the rocky outcrop, the view became shrouded in mist. The wind rushed through the trees and roared every now and then; and the distant waves crashed against the harbour wall in Paleokastritsa. A bald man with a beard skipped to a higher rock for a better view. My heart leapt. He was within an inch of the afterlife.

Down the path came Simo and his cousin, bearing what looked like cushions or mattresses encased in plastic. On closer inspection, I realised that it was bread, loaves of bread, and lots of them.

When the service finished, a surge of people entered the chapel, to kiss the icon and take the blessed bread. I filed around but neither kissed nor took.

Up on the path, Ilias dispensed sweet bread loaves and pots of nuts and seeds which he gave us to take. It was his wife's church, after all. There was nothing the priest could say about it.

Along the donkey track, people made their way back to the village. Cars passed and tooted at us, and there were shouts of '*Xronia polla!*' But when the priest went by, he turned his car stereo to the pop music channel and looked straight ahead. But despite his coldness, something had happened at St Simeon.

Among the villagers, we had been accepted; and I did not feel quite so lonely as I had before.

Down in the *plateia*, we met Antonis and congratulated him on the work he and his family had done to brighten up the church for its name day. And we told him we had heard the story about why the church had been built.

'Ah, that story,' he said, with a look that suggested we were born yesterday. 'There are stories like that all over Greece.'

In a telephone call from the agent, we learned that we had to decorate not just the walls and ceilings of the Villa Oleander but the doors, window frames and kitchen cupboards too. The work was mounting up. It was going to be a bigger job than we thought. Picking up the paint from Corfu Town, we consoled ourselves with the fact that it was St Valentine's Day and we were going out for a meal that evening. But before then there was an exchange of presents. Andreas handed me a card and a pair of men's socks. I gave him two pairs of socks, some moisturiser and a card hastily made out of a sheet of A4 paper with a message written in black magic marker. And who said romance was dead?

We climbed into the car and headed for Corfu Town and two drinks on the Liston. We planned to go to The Rex, a pukka restaurant we had only heard about but never eaten in. But when we got there, all the tables were occupied. Back on the road home, we stopped off at Kontokali and the Bistro Boileau; but they were busy until at least ten o'clock. So we went a bit further along the road and found a place at the Chinese restaurant, had a nice meal and then cracked open our fortune cookies in a place now full of romantic Greeks.

'*A bird in the hand is better than a feather in the air.*' Did that mean I needed to get on and finish at least one of these books rather than having three unfinished ones flitting up and down like a child's mobile?

Meanwhile, my husband's said, '*A friend in the market is better than money in the purse.*'

On the way home, a hare lolloped across the road. It looked up at us as if to say, *Slow down and enjoy the ride.* We pressed onwards and missed the turning to our village and headed down to Paleokastritsa. It was empty, devoid of tourists and devoid of life. We parked up and got out, the waves rustling gently over the pebbles down on the beach. In the black sky, a new moon was joined by the brightest stars I had ever seen. An owl let out a series of high-pitched, monotone hoots and then a donkey walked down from the monastery.

It was raining again. The water would be burbling through the streets of Corfu Town, chasing itself along shiny pavements and down into storm drains and then up again in a never-ending game of tag.

February is a chilly and wet old month in Corfu.

'Him the coldest,' Spiros Bear told us, as we stood next to our diminishing log pile. 'You need more wood for fire.'

So he ordered a load for us and a ton arrived the next day. It was olive wood, which burns well as soon as it is cut, unlike other wood which needs to be seasoned before you can use it. Olive trees are protected in Corfu, which stems from the Venetians who passed a law forbidding the felling of them. We had heard of poor people from Thessaly who had been discovered chopping down olive trees on the sacred slopes of Mount Olympus. These were tough times in Greece, with power cuts, strikes and high energy bills becoming increasingly common.

In Corfu, there was an irony in that an empty store bearing the name *Euro Town* was near-derelict while up the road, *China City* – with its rows of jogging pants and dubious tops with seams that broke as soon as you looked at them – was booming.

On the surface though, life seemed to go on as normal in the villages. Work was precious, wages were low and bills were high. In the *kafenio*, the old men played cards while another group turned over from the news, with its hectoring politicians and footage repeated over and over again, to the National Geographic channel. Lions mating was of much more interest than austerity measures. There was only so much austerity people could stomach.

'The people are angry,' Kiki told us. 'It is the ordinary people who suffer. They do not like it that the rich people do not pay their taxes or put it in a bank in Switzerland and it is the ordinary people who pay the price. They are angry at the politicians who have allowed this to happen.'

We were driving out of the village when we first saw them: pick-up trucks piled high with bags fit to burst, with waggy-tailed dogs pacing up and down in the back, smiling in excitement. We followed them up the hill and out across to the straggling village of Vistonas, where a ramshackle collection of buildings topped by a mixture of tiled and corrugated iron roofs appeared to be the centre of the trucks' universe. Through the bare branches we glimpsed the cab of an old Mercedes lorry, its other end obscured.

We parked the car and got out. The air was steeped in the strong and bitter smell of olives. A truck reversed and stopped at the entrance to a small factory where the driver got out and took the sacks off the back. We ventured in and asked if we could stand and watch. The proprietor, another Spiros, was quite happy to explain the entire process.

The black olives were poured from sacks into a hopper and taken on an incredible journey in which they were shaken and washed and crushed and steeped and shaken again to become a golden liquid, thick and pungent, rich and natural, at the other side of the building. The Alfa-Laval machinery, bright green and gleaming steel, clanged and spun and whirred as it was fed with the olives. The whole thing was like a Mediterranean version of *Charlie and the Chocolate Factory*. Down a chute the olives went. and then up a steep conveyor belt before being shaken and washed and whooshed off to the macerator, where each section was labelled with the name of a customer on a chalk board to avoid getting the wrong batch at the business end.

The pulp shot off to the press, with the residue whizzing upwards and out into the open air. Back inside, the golden nectar that was pure olive oil poured out into a container of shiny steel. The oil was weighed and poured, *glug-glug-glug*, into massive containers; and then the customer put it back on the pick-up truck to take home. But not before he had ambled across to a central table for a bit of Feta sprinkled with paprika, some crusty bread soaked in fresh olive oil and a plastic cup or two of home-made wine.

94

'Here, you have some,' Spiros the Olive Man said in Greek. As we had learned, it would have been rude to refuse. You do not turn your nose up at hospitality. You receive it with a smile and wide open arms.

The place was buzzing with machinery and new arrivals. And then in came Turkey Spiros, with his matinée idol looks, smartly pressed trousers, shiny shoes and a truck full of olives. He flashed us a huge grin, greeting us like an old friend, and made the *kafenio* sign for drink. A drink? Of course.

So there we stood, joining in this simple olive harvest feast with relative strangers. It felt good.

Part III

Spring

And yet, perchance in this sea-trancèd isle
Chewing the bitter fruit of memory
Some God lies hidden in the asphodel.

Oscar Wilde, *Santa Decca*

March

With the start of a new month, the damp air lifted to reveal a warmth that seeped into our bones. We still needed a log fire in the evening but it seemed as if we had turned a corner, both in terms of the weather and our relationship. We rolled up our sleeves and got on with the decorating to the soundtrack of hits from the Seventies. I was still homesick but at last I was coming to terms with it. Moping is an energy sapper and I was fed up with it. I knew our year away was the opportunity of a lifetime yet I had wasted months of it by pining for something I had left behind. Just weeks into our Corfu adventure I had come to realise the grass wasn't greener, it was just a different shade.

Now, the shooting season was at an end and our wake-up calls consisted of the yelling of a thousand cockerels, the ricocheting cackle of the geese next door telling each other dirty jokes, crying cats that sounded like frightened children and the persistent dawn chorus of the dogs chained up on patches of land all across the valley. As I looked out from the balcony at the sun coming up and throwing its light onto the mountain behind Skripero, it occurred to me that Odysseus and I had something in common. Like the Greek hero, here I was, in Calypso's thrall on this most beautiful of islands but desperate to go home. For Odysseus, home meant the bare and rocky island of Ithaca which, by Ionian standards, Homer rated as pretty poor. For me, home meant green fields and hedges, wind-sculpted beech trees, muddy gateways and mist. Yes, I was even homesick for mist. I'd look out of my window and my view of the mountain, covered in ribbons of low cloud and say to myself: *Yes, but it's not like the mist we get at home.* There hadn't been any monsters to contend with on my journey so far, not on the scale of the terrors that had faced Odysseus at least. But there was a constant temptation to go onto Facebook and gaze with envy at the photographs my friends were posting of scenes back home. I had set up a website for the village shortly after moving to

Corfu and I was always updating it, reminding myself of what I was missing. It was as if I was Odysseus lashed to the mast and listening to the song of the sirens.

Homesickness had been holding me tightly in its grasp, gripping my insides as if I hadn't eaten for days. It hurt, physically. I would look out at the mountains from the balcony and feel enclosed, trapped. They were bearing down on me and I couldn't breathe. And I had put this feeling firmly at the feet of the man who had brought me here, as if I hadn't had any input into the process of coming away, despite giving up my job and coming away. I was deluding myself; it wasn't his fault; we had done this together; we were in this together. And then I thought, how could I feel like this, in such a beautiful place, the land of the lotus eaters? Especially when all over the world, and particularly Greece, there were people suffering, *really* suffering. I had no right to feel this way. And there was only one person who could sort it out, and that person was me. I had to sort it; I had to acknowledge that yes, this was the way I felt, but I didn't need to feel guilty about feeling homesick, it was just how I was and I had to live with it. It was important now for me to make the best of what most people would give their right arm for. It was time to live in the present rather than think about what new life I was going to carve out for myself when our year away had ended.

I sat down at my writing desk and got out a sheet of A4 paper and a magic marker from the drawer. The blank space in front of me was not going to scare me. It would help me sort out my direction. Once upon a time I would have used tarot cards to divine my future path. But putting my faith in superstition was no good; I needed a practical solution. So I did what I had done for the last few years when I was faced with an impasse in my life, and I drew up a list of bullet points, in date order, of all the things I wanted to get done and of all the places I wanted to see during our remaining months here. It was ordered and it was how I worked best. Spontaneity is all very well but sometimes you need a plan to achieve it. And once I had my list right there in front of me, I was able to see where I wanted to be by the time our year was up. There were books to finish, writing competitions to enter, photographs to take. There were freelancing leads to follow up, work in the house and in the garden to finish. And there was a life to have here before I even thought of going back. And dance, I really wanted to dance.

'You seem a little bit happier,' Andreas said to me, as we tucked into octopus in red sauce at The Three Brothers one Sunday.

And I was. Because now I had my head sorted out. Weekdays were for working and weekends were for leisure and maybe speaking to the grandchildren on Skype. What remained of this year out was for exploration and, I hoped, discovery.

As a country child, I was used to lush scenery and the change of the seasons. But nothing had prepared me for the beauty of the Corfu olive groves in spring. It was here that a sense of place finally gripped me, the mountains surrounding the village becoming a protective arm and no longer hemming me in. Great drifts of white daisies mingled with swathes of small and delicate pink geraniums. Here and there were solitary anemones, cerise and upright, their petals around a dark centre as if drawn by a child. Miniature irises bloomed like military wives waiting for their menfolk to return. Fields of asphodel, such a potent symbol in Greek mythology's view of the afterlife, lay before me. And here among the asphodel's spikes was the most beautiful cow I had ever seen, horned and tethered, sleek, serene and solitary, chewing the cud on the fresh grass. The cow, a heifer, was light brown and had a gorgeous, soft face. Although the wrong colour, I imagined her as Io, the nymph Zeus seduced and then turned into a white heifer to keep her hidden from Hera, his wife. But the goddess, who was also Zeus's sister and well used to her husband's philandering, wasn't fooled and sent a gadfly to torment her. Io fled and kicked her way around the Mediterranean, landing, it is said, in a sea that was named the Ionian in her honour, before finally arriving in Egypt.

Spring had arrived in Corfu. Carpets of flowers were at my feet, on the roadsides and in any nook or cranny open to the elements. Violets smiled sweetly and astonishing heads of comfrey nodded in agreement. There were vast clumps of wild honesty so purple they could have belonged to royalty. Grape hyacinths, jonquils marched across swampy fields and great yellow flowers from the pea family lurked in clumps, waiting to pounce. Euphorbia was euphoric in sulphur yellow shouty-ness while variegated thistle stalked the ground, SAS-style, concealing its spikes beneath.

To be in Greece at this time of year was like nowhere else on Earth. It has more species of flowering plants and ferns than any other country in Europe. There are some 6,000: six times more than France and making the British Isle's 2,300 seem paltry by comparison. According to Hellmut Baumann in his book *Greek Wild Flowers and Plant Lore in Ancient Greece*, 'Nowhere in Europe have conditions been more favourable for the development of such rich flora. This is due to diverse combinations of geological, topographical and climatological conditions'.

But little would the summer visitor to Greece, and indeed Corfu, know of such richness. By the time the Easy Jet flights touched down on to the airport's hot tarmac, most of the flowers would be gone, leaving the spotlight to those blousy exotics, the jacaranda, bougainvillea and oleander, together with assorted litter strewn along the verges.

I stopped to notice the detail on the blooms and longed to know what some of the common names might be. I thought of my mother who had taught me so much about the wild flowers I grew up with in the West Country, such as gypsy lace, which most people know as cow parsley, and the deadnettle and the tiny ballet pumps hidden inside its flowers, which were always available for the fairies when they had danced holes in their own shoes during the night. There were similar stories about the flowers in Corfu. But these were rooted in mythology rather than the whims of an over-imaginative mother. On the larkspur flower, for example, you could see a letter A, flanked on both sides by an I in memory of the hero Aias (Ajax) who threw himself on his own sword after losing to Odysseus in a quarrel over who should inherit the armour of Achilles. '*Ai*' is also the Greek cry of anguish and mourning.

The wild flowers made me happy to be alive. With spring came new beginnings.

It was a bank holiday weekend in Corfu Town as the island prepared to usher in Clean Monday. It marked the beginning of

102

Lent, when Greeks celebrate the fast and welcome the dawn of spring.

A van stuffed full of artichokes was parked just up from the AB supermarket. A man in the old town sold large shrimps, still wriggling, from a basket. There was bunting hanging across the streets and a civilised demonstration by young Communists outside the bank. The smell of freshly-baked bread pulled pedestrians in from the pavements and into the bakery. Two South American men set up on the pavement and the ubiquitous sound of amplified Andean panpipes wafted up the street, past a beggar boy holding out a Kentucky Fried Chicken box with a few cents inside. A couple of doorsteps up were his mother and sister, hands out for money, while further along was the Corfu bag lady, who, as usual, sat asleep in a shop doorway, with her parka hood up and sunglasses on. She never collected anything but bags. The town eccentric, wearing a long, blonde curly wig, clutched red and white cuddly toys and ribbons around his ample girth. A music student practised the piano behind an open window. The queue in the fruit shop, where navel oranges were about eighty cents a kilo, seemed nine kilometres long. A small, masked parade appeared from nowhere and strolled out of sight along the street.

There was a sense of anticipation in the air as the town and villages of the island prepared for carnival. With austerity measures, locals said carnival was not what it used to be. But there was always room to enjoy simply being alive.

In the old town, a swallow flew over the sea wall and was joined by six more, dipping and diving and laughing. They had arrived. Swallows and wild flowers: the harbingers of spring.

In the village that evening, the children got hold of the bell ropes, Lovejoy and a man dressed in a cow onesie helped grill the *souvlaki* and I took the laptop around the *plateia* so that my granddaughter back in the UK could see what it was like.

'This is the square – we call it the *plateia* in Greece,' I said to the screen. 'And this is the *kafenio* and mini-market.'

Oh, the wonders of modern technology. Connected to the shop's broadband, I could even show her the cheese on the deli counter and Kiki weighing it out.

Spiros Ron looked over my shoulder at the screen and said, '*Kalispera*.' He smiled that twinkly Spiros Ron smile at me and said, '*Poli orea*,' – very beautiful. I was sharing this moment with my girl. I was no longer sick for home but pleased to think she would be here for a week in the summer so I could show her what it was like. Back out in the *plateia*, there was a rowdy clamour as a piñata – a papier-mâché container fashioned by a creative parent into the shape of a clown's face – was lowered from one of the trees. A group of children in fancy dress stood in a circle while a blindfolded girl dressed as Snow White bashed the air with a baseball bat, until a father took over and beat the piñata to a pulp. A shower of sweets descended, as did the children into a sort of scrum, the ones at the bottom of the heap yelling and crying out for help.

'That looks fun,' my granddaughter said. 'Will I be able to do that when I come out?'

The DJ turned the music up and the children leapt up and danced to 'Gangnam Style.'

'I really like the look of that, Granny,' my granddaughter said. And then the connection went.

Daylight faded and turned into night. At what would have been way past the bedtimes of English children, the children were still tearing around the trees, dancing, cycling and playing tag. When Turkish music wove its way around the *plateia*, a complaint was made to the DJ.

'This is Greece,' said Spiros Bear's brother Lambis. 'We do not want Turkish music here.'

When the appropriate music came on, Lambis pulled me up from my chair.

'We dance,' he said. He danced all over the world. He had once performed at Sidmouth Folk Festival, which is held annually in a seaside town not far away from where we lived in Dorset. For many years, our village had a coach trip to the festival. I could have even seen Lambis performing and not known it.

Outside the *kafenio*, he showed me his moves. I watched, counted his steps and followed.

'No,' Lambis said, rather impatiently. 'You have to *feel* the music.'

I shut everything out of my head apart from the melody and stopped concentrating. I let the tune seep into me and just *danced*. The graceful steps came from nowhere, echoing Lambis's for the most part, and applause broke out around me. My partner was pleased with his pupil. 'This is your first lesson,' he said.

We sat down and Lambis introduced us to a large, yellowing moustache trying its best to conceal the bulk of a smiling, elderly man called Nikos. His English stretched to 'very good' and 'problem'.

'When he was younger, Nikos was great dancer, much better than me,' Lambis said. 'He could do the scissors.'

Nikos winked at me. 'Very good,' he said. 'Problem.'

He got up with Lambis to perform a sedate and graceful dance. It reminded me of a pair of pigeons performing a mating ritual on the Liston.

The music changed to 1970s disco. Lambis introduced us to his other friend, a slim, middle-aged woman who was very pleasant but seemed rather lethargic as she sucked heavily on a cigarette. As the bottles of Retsina – Lambis's favourite tipple – stacked up on the table, the woman followed me as I got up to dance to 'Saturday Night Fever'. I thought I was doing well and then I saw her out of the corner of my eye.

She was truly the greatest disco dancer I had ever seen.

She threw shapes in a sort of John Travolta-meets-robot kind of way right across the *plateia*. The woman was on fire. A large circle formed around her as we attempted to mimic her movements.

And then the firecrackers went off and Andreas came back from the outside toilet, a quivering wreck.

'You've missed the best bit,' I said, pointing to Lambis's friend. 'This woman is absolutely incredible.'

'I couldn't get out,' he said. 'Didn't you hear the noise?'

'The firecrackers?'

'Yes,' he said, mopping his brow. 'Spiros Ron's grandson was letting them off outside the toilet door.'

The DJ put on The Village People so we got up and led Lambis, the world's greatest disco dancer and two small children in the 'YMCA' dance routine. That night, the music went on into the small hours. In neighbouring Gardelades it was still going strong when we woke up just after six the next morning.

Dressed in old layers, we continued to decorate inside, do the gardening and move a delivery of logs to join the neat pile that we had already stacked next to the house. We noticed that Spiros Bear's wood pile – which had been just that: a pile – was beginning to look neat and tidy like ours. It was still cold but on the days when the sun came out, we could feel the warmth just waiting to burst forth and multiply.

At the *plateia*, Yannis of the Mohican and White Sunglasses rattled up on his clapped-out scooter, with six cuttings from his grapevine for us to plant. Staying astride the machine, he handed them to us. The bike had no stand so he never got off it. It was more holes than metal and we would frequently see him in the *plateia*, waiting for someone to arrive who could go in and get him a packet of cigarettes. It was a clear day, with a beautiful, blue Corfu sky enveloping us in loveliness. It was a promising start, because we were leaving the village for a week and heading for the mainland to see what lay beyond the Corfu Channel and the snow-capped mountains. But before we set off, Turkey Spiros insisted on buying us a coffee, as did Kiki. We sloshed back to the house to plant the vines. The washing billowed on the line.

A head appeared above the wall, accompanied by a gruff voice.

'What you doing?'

We told Spiros Bear we were preparing for a week's adventure in northern Greece.

'I look after house for you,' he said, as he walked in through the gate, a lumbering Defa following close behind. 'She pregnant.'

I had only just noticed her swollen belly.

Spiros made a clicking noise with his teeth. Evidently the father was a large dog from up the road who came calling while Defa was on her own.

'Him bad dog,' he said. 'I worry for her.'

On television, it appeared that Golden Dawn was giving away food to poor people. Anything for popularity. It did not bode well. I wished that Greece would make a stand and do something about this hateful political party, which preyed on the fears of desperate people.

At the port, we bought a discounted ticket for locals and drove on to the ferry, *Kerkyra*. Two minutes after we had found a seat, the boat set sail, heading down past the pretty waterfront of Corfu Town and its twin fortresses and across the channel to the hills beyond. It is a journey that takes about an hour-and-a-half and opens up a land very different to Corfu. After disembarking at Igoumenitsa, we drove up the gloriously quiet Egnatia Highway to Metsovo, which glowed in the afternoon sun, with snow on the mountains above. The skiing season was near its end but we were able to hire a skidoo for half an hour. The snow was glossy, like a meringue. Exhilarated, my husband alighted from the machine with tears in his eyes.

'That was wonderful,' he said. 'I've always wanted to do that. I felt like James Bond.'

So we handed over some more euros and did it again.

The north of Greece is a beautiful, wild, surprising place and so close to Corfu. From the lovely villages in the Pindos mountains to the treasures that lie beyond the new road, it is a magical trip: a road less travelled, especially out of season.

From Metsovo we headed through wild bear country to the Greek region of Macedonia, up into the hills to Nympheo, a village rich in history and money. It was a favourite with Vlach merchants who traded in gold, silver, tobacco and cotton. Their families lived in Nympheo, safe and hidden from the valley floor. Today, properties in the village have been bought and restored by wealthy professionals. It is an oasis of tranquillity. We liked it very much. After a walk around its quiet, cobbled streets, which had a deep layer of snow at each side, we headed back to our guest house and our warm, friendly hosts, Yannis, Roula and Hermes the Chow, who was more like a big teddy bear than a dog.

It was one of those bed and breakfast places we had booked through the internet and hoped for the best. It couldn't have been better. Sitting down in a room overlooking the village, the roofs of the houses covered in snow, we were presented with a hearty meal cooked with love by the shy Roula. We crumbled Feta into our thick, golden vegetable soup, dipping in great hunks of home-made bread. It was followed by fat, honey-glazed lamb shanks with home-made chips and shredded white cabbage salad, accompanied by deep red, full-bodied wine from the Naoussa winery. For dessert, we feasted on cored apple rings, drizzled with cinnamon and sugar syrup, and preserved quince.

After a very comfortable night's sleep, we threw open the curtains to soak up the view of the village rooftops in the snow. After a breakfast of fresh orange juice, rice pudding, ham and cheese omelette, cheese pies, bread, mandarin and kiwi fruit marmalades and coffee, Yannis took us on a tour of this lovely village.

'I will drive you,' he said. 'Before it starts to snow again.'

We had approximately two hours, he reckoned, before a blizzard was due. If we didn't leave that day, we would be there for the rest of the week. Confident behind the wheel of his large 4x4, he told us he had been a retail manager for a large company and had always been away from home a lot, travelling. Before the economic crisis began, he and his Crete-born wife decided to pack in the rat race and sink their savings into the guest house, which they had lovingly and carefully restored. We hoped in these times of austerity that people would still find their way to Nympheo and avail themselves of its charms.

The track to the nearby bear sanctuary was full of ruts and potholes but the occupants were still hibernating and dead to the world, the only evidence of their existence being the strong smell of bear dung. It was on then to the church, which was undergoing an expensive restoration funded by the village's wealthy inhabitants. Yannis introduced us to an old school friend, another Yannis, a forty-something priest with a woolly hat and beard, a twinkle in his eyes and a wonderful, welcoming smile. In his black robes, he padded around in trainers, showing us around the building and taking us upstairs into his office. He produced two ancient wedding crowns, some of the few things to have survived a disastrous fire, and placed them on our heads. Our host Yannis translated.

'He says he could marry you again here. You know, renew your vows.'

I was rather taken aback. Having been on the verge of separating just before Christmas, renewing our wedding vows was the furthest thing from my mind. Papas Yannis's attitude and demeanour were so different to those of our own village priest back in Corfu. He radiated goodness and openness: a calm, gentle, patient, beautiful person. A cabinet maker by trade, he was called to the priesthood at the age of forty-three. Whatever your beliefs, you always meet some people in this life who are innately good. A look, a word or a touch are all you need to feel connected to their serene spirituality. Papas Yannis is such a person. I made a mental note to go back one day.

With a snowstorm on its way, we pushed on, to Edessa and its waterfalls, to Veria and its stunning collection of grave goods, statues, pots and brightly coloured jewellery, before heading for Vergina, Mount Olympus and Meteora.

It is an isolated spot, like a forgotten Wild West town. But two hundred schoolchildren getting on assorted buses in the car park indicated this was some kind of mecca, even out of season. Ahead of us, a party of German tourists was escorted into a low dome of grass via a tunnel. It was one of those heart-in-the-mouth moments. Would it be worth the detour? Could Andreas put up with yet another museum?

Vergina transported us back to more than 350 years BC, to the time of Alexander the Great and his father, Philip II of Macedonia. Just like spring in Corfu, Vergina took me completely by surprise. Even Andreas, who always preferred to hang out with the living rather than the ancient dead, walked around with mouth agape.

In 1977, the Greek archaeologist Manolis Andronikos made a spectacular discovery. Vergina had long been of interest to ancient historians who thought it could be the site of the ancient city of Aigai, the first capital of the Kingdom of Macedonia. This was the spot where in 336 BC Philip II was murdered at his daughter's wedding and where his son Alexander the Great was proclaimed king. The first excavations took place in the 19th century, with more being carried out in the 1930s, 50s and 60s. One of the most important finds was the monumental palace, sadly closed when we called in. This was a disappointment, yes, but our pilgrimage was more than rewarded when we trailed behind the party of Germans. This is the spot where Andronikos decided to excavate a large tumulus. It turned out to be one of the archaeological finds of the century and certainly the most important in Greece in the 20th century. He had discovered The Royal Tombs of Vergina.

We walked through the tunnel into darkness, where, despite the buzz of the German tourists ahead, a kind of spiritual silence descended on us. It was not long before we were on our own and able to stroll around in awe at Andronikos' discoveries. We were inside the tumulus, where four elaborate royal tombs were on display in the positions they had been found. Incredibly preserved wall paintings, including one depicting the rape of Persephone by Hades, adorned these graves. In one of the tombs, the bones of a man had been found in a solid gold casket. They were identified as belonging to Philip II, the great powerhouse of Macedonia who coined the saying 'divide and conquer'. The scholars can't agree, however, with some of them arguing that the bones belonged to his son, Philip Arrhidaeus. Whatever the grave's provenance, the splendour of Vergina is mind-blowing, with the most beautiful golden artefacts on display, shining like suns in the neutral, dark setting of the museum. A delicate, intricate crown of oak leaves and acorns was found in the casket with the bones and makes a striking display in a glass case. It is mirrored on the other side of the room by a wreath of golden myrtle, found with the bones of a woman, thought to have been Philip's favourite wife. Her fate would have been to have burned with her husband's body on his funeral pyre.

Glad that we had ventured on to the Greek mainland to savour some of its rich offerings, we left Vergina, stopping off to say hello to the gods at Mount Olympus, only to be thwarted by snow before we could reach the Plateau of the Muses, where I was hoping to find inspiration. We took solace in the fact that we had booked ourselves into a spa hotel by the coast, incredibly

110

cheap because it was out of season. From our room, which included jacuzzi and log fire, we could see the snow-topped mountain, the throne of Zeus, which rose so majestically on the skyline. It was on, then, to one of the most breathtaking places on earth, Meteora. From the flat plans of Thessaly, the incredible rock pinnacles came into view. It is a strange place, like something from the set of a science fiction film or the movie *Black Narcissus* in which Deborah Kerr leads a repressed kind of existence as a nun who in the climax faces the dark jealousy of mentally unstable Sister Ruth. Right at the top of these geological wonders, which appear to reach up to the sky, are the monasteries. From the 11th century onwards monks have been coming here, leading a life of hermitage and solitude, although these days the tourist buses are frequent visitors.

The piety and devotion in the Greek Orthodox Church are something to behold at Meteora. It must have required almost superhero effort to build on these slender outcrops. How anyone scaled to the top in the first place defies belief. Inside, the simple interiors are painted richly with icons from the Byzantine era and radiate a sense of calm, overlooking a plain on which the people and their homes are like ants.

Our bank, The Bank of Cyprus, was in terrible trouble. We'd had to get a bank account to enable us to become tenants of the Villa Oleander and we'd been advised that the bank was as good as any. But at the end of March, a 10 million euro international bailout of Cyprus was announced, in exchange for the bank being closed. Large scale investors were taxed, many of them Russians but including some British ex-pats who had entrusted all their life savings to this well-known bank. Luckily, we had put as little as possible in it and were not affected. But it was a sobering thought that at any time Greece could go completely tits up.

Back in Corfu Town, the storms whipped up the sea and the road was flooded at Garitsa Bay. Great waves lashed the sea wall and smashed into the windscreen. Down below the old fort, the few boats in the water were pummelled, swaying precariously and in danger of sinking.

We got back to the village to the news that poor Defa had died. She'd had a belly full of dead puppies inside her and had had gone into a coma and never recovered. Spiros Bear was beside himself.

'She was too young and too small,' he said.

He buried her on a plot of land where his parents used to have a house.

'She was good dog.'

April

I had a friend in the UK whose favourite phrase was 'never turn down an invitation'. It became something of a family mantra and, coupled with my favourite advertising slogan, 'just do it', led to some interesting situations. We made a point of always being open to new ideas and experiences.

Late one morning, we received a text out of the blue:

> *What are you doing this evening?*
> *How about a mandolin concert?*

We'd been planning to spend the balmy evening eating squid with wild asparagus, which we'd bought from the market. We were going to sit on our own terrace, looking out on a newly-cleared garden, our reward for a week of hard work. Not that looking at on logs was the prettiest of views but it was very satisfying.

Instead, we heeded the family mantra and ended up enjoying *pastitsio* at the home of Gorgeous George and his wife, The Graceful Mrs George, who had one of the finest views of the island. We looked out across to the old fort of Corfu Town in the far distance and down south to the hills beyond. Straight ahead we saw the sails of a yacht beating up the coast towards the marina at Gouvia.

And then it was off to The Graceful Mrs George's church community centre, which looked nothing from the outside, as the traffic raced past on the main road from Corfu Town to Paleokastritsa. But inside, it was a little oasis, with a coffee bar, toddlers' play area, table tennis table for the older children, comfy seats and books.

Next door was a smart little hall used for all sorts of events and live performances.

As we sat down, we were not sure what to expect. And then they came on, the young mandolin players of Corfu, the Mantolinata Menestrelli.

Eight young people played mandolins, accompanied by two guitars and keyboards, playing the music of their homeland. And then, behind us, members of the audience began to sing with tuneful and hearty voices to the chorus of 'Kerkyra'. It comes from the credit sequence of the 1972 film, *The Countess of Corfu*, which stars the island's most famous actress, the late Rena Vlahopoulou. Written by George Katsaros, this pop song has become something of an island favourite, sung more often than 'Never on a Sunday'. Rena declares her love for the island through the catchy refrain (*'Kerkyra! Kerkyra!'*) and references to well-known place names. Its English translation, according to the Dorset/Corfu scholar Jim Potts, goes something like this:

> The tastiest young girls
> I saw in Paleokastritsa
> And the freshest fish are found
> only in Benitsa

'Did you enjoy it?' The Graceful Mrs George asked at the end of the performance.

Enjoy it? We loved it. Never turn down an invitation was a good motto to live by.

As Greek Easter approached, about as late as this moveable feast could ever be, Corfu became busier with the start of the holiday season. There were aeroplanes in the sky and cruise ships in the harbour. At first, the island was slow to wake up to these new visitors, who wandered around forlorn because everything seemed to be closed. But now there were tables on the pavements outside the tavernas and waiters touting for business.

There were irritating and leggy teenage British girls, singing One Direction songs in the queue at the Lidl checkout with their mother, their shorts so short you could see the cheeks of their bottoms and probably more if you looked a little closer. There were sunburnt families wandering around the resorts, amazed that the Greeks were still in thick coats and knee-high boots.

Coaches lined the Spianada and fake lamb carcasses spun on spits in the barbecue shop. The streets of old Corfu Town became a language hotch-potch, as the tourists wandered aimlessly past the nick-nack shops selling trinkets made in Vietnam and windows full of icons of saints they had never heard of.

We dived down an alleyway overlooked by a string of Greek flags and clothes on a washing line. We were heading for an unprepossessing little place, a mere hole in the wall, the existence of which was marked only by a large, cuddly toy dog, sitting on a chair outside and with a red heart around its neck. The tourists didn't give it a second glance.

'You must go there,' Spiros the Bear had told us the previous night as he played cards in the *kafenio*. 'It is best *souvlakia* in Corfu.'

'Yes,' said Spiros Waiter. 'Him very fat man. Yesterday him go to Corfu Towns and have thirty.'

To emphasise his point, he licked his finger and wrote 3-0 on the *kafenio* table.

'And him have two portion fries.'

This was Greek exaggeration, of course. We knew our Spiros did not like chips. But it was quite conceivable that he could manage thirty *souvlakia* at one sitting, although he strongly denied it.

'Him is wrong. I have six *souvlakia*. Them is good. The fat, it makes them taste more better.'

He paused for a moment, to savour the memory. It was clear that this was a place we needed to visit. So the next day, we found the toy dog and went inside to sit at one of the four tables crammed in one next to the other. There was a large, swarthy man building up the heat on the grill with an electric hairdryer, as *souvlakia* were cooked to order. We asked a plump, smiling woman we took to be his wife for the menu. She pointed to the wall. We could have *souvlaki*, chips, bread and feta with olive oil and paprika. That was it. That was the extent of the menu. So we sipped on ouzo and waited for our feast to arrive.

When our eight *souvlakia* arrived, they turned out to be the tastiest in the ten years or more we had been visiting Greece. And we would never know why.

115

'It is, what you say, a secret,' said a man on the table next to us. 'Every *souvlaki* different in every place. This is best. I am forty-eight and remember I come here as little boy. Always queues and sometimes the people fight.'

He looked around him at the faded decor and, with his foot, shooed two pigeons out of the shop. And he threw a look at the man in charge of the grill, who had put his glass of retsina under the counter for safekeeping as he tizzled up yet more *souvlakia*. Our cook shared his name with the brave King of Sparta, Leonidas, who had led the ill-fated mission of the three hundred against the mighty Xerxes, King of Persia. Every now and then in Greece, links with the ancient past sprang up where you least expected it.

'It is always the same, it has not changed,' the long-standing customer said about the shop. And then he grinned. 'Except maybe the *souvlakia* are smaller.'

With the change in the weather came new life.

New flowers replaced the geranium and daisies. Scabious popped up by the roadside and the purple honesty turned into crimson purses, ready to reveal thirty pieces of silver later in the year. As Greek Easter approached, the vibrant purplish-pink flowers of the Judas Tree blossomed on bare branches before the lime green, kidney-shaped leaves appeared. The trees were all over the island, vast swathes of colour in a sea of olive green. Judas Iscariot was said to have hanged himself from a tree like this after denouncing Jesus. According to legend, the flowers were originally pale and blushed pink with shame. Another version was that the flowers represent Judas's entrails. The locals called the tree something completely different and had never heard of the Judas connection.

Whatever the story behind them, they were a striking sight.

Elsewhere, the wisteria grew so vigorously, it romped up telegraph poles to look like trees. On closer inspection, some of them *were* trees. The orange began to blossom and its heady scent spread across the roads of our village, mixed with the aroma of moussaka and *souvlaki* from the tavernas in the *plateia*.

And in Corfu Town, the cricket pitch on the Spianada was having a haircut.

116

Down at the market, fish with wings and fish with stern faces lay alongside things with tentacles and crabs with blue legs. Shrimps still alive sprung from their polystyrene boxes and brushed against gurnards, bream, monkfish, John Dory and tuna.

The courgettes were small and sweet, with firm flowers still attached and not an earwig in sight. The purple artichoke heads screamed: *'Eat us, eat us! You know we are worth the trouble.'*

'Let's go to that stall,' I said, pointing to a small stand crammed with fruit and vegetables and manned by a tiny woman in her late fifties with thick, shoulder-length hair and gaps in her teeth.

'Why that one?' Andreas said.

'Well, the veg are good. And she looks like she comes from Beaminster.'

He strolled up to the woman and puffed himself out, pointing at the courgettes and asking in English but with a Greek accent for a kilo of courgettes.

She gave him two kilos and poked him in the stomach and then gave him two artichokes *for luck*. She pointed at herself and said, 'Me, Eleni,' and then grabbed my husband and did a little dance as the shoppers bustled by.

We had found our friend in the market. The fortune cookie on St Valentine's Day had been spot on. It was better than money in the purse.

There was a metallic *trundling* sound coming down our driveway.

It was Spiros Bear's brother-in-law, Smiling Ilia, who had arrived to rotavate a patch of our garden. With all the clearing done and the official end of the bonfire season just passed, we were ready to cultivate. The previous day, we had asked tentatively if he would be able to do it for us after we spotted him clearing the ground beneath his vines. He was in like a shot and would not take any money for doing it. All he asked for was a ladder to go up into our palm tree, where angels feared to tread, to cut the young fronds and extract the white shoots to make the crosses for Palm Sunday at the weekend. He had about four words of English: 'good', 'very good' and 'coffee' so, at the end of his session with the Merry Tiller, he uttered all four. After coffee on the terrace, where the Sicilian sweet peas I had planted a fortnight ago were romping heavenwards to meet the vine emerging overhead, we strolled up to the *kafenio* and mini-market and took our pick from all the plants outside, at fifty or sixty cents a pot. We bought watermelon and cantaloupe to put in, courgette, three varieties of pepper, white aubergine and black aubergine, red and green basil, cucumber and two types of tomato.

The pattern of the day had changed, now that the sun was out and temperatures were hitting 26.5 degrees centigrade at ten thirty in the morning. The warm evenings were ideal for planting and there was a real sense of anticipation in the air and in the ground. The card players came to the *kafenio* later in the evening after a day of preparing their patches of land for planting.

There was also a sense of anticipation in our house as our first visitors were due to arrive from Dorset, just in time for Easter and the blooming of our prolific mock orange blossom. Crisp white sheets dried on the washing line in a beautiful warm breeze, while pillows and duvets aired on the upstairs balcony. The second half of our year was almost here, with at least six lots of visitors lined up over the coming months.

In the village church, the palm crosses hung from the chandeliers. A smiling villager called Theodoros, the one who looked like Matt Monro, was in harmonic form as he chanted at the front. At the end of the service, the priest handed out palm crosses and posies. But I decided - following my experience at Epiphany - to leave by the back door, avoid humiliation, and not collect one. We were a little disappointed, as the palm fronds had come from our own tree. But there was no good to be had in labouring the point, in case we were snubbed again. So we exchanged kindly smiles with the village congregation and headed for Corfu Town and the Palm Sunday parade.

We parked on the road to the market, just as a coach ahead caused a traffic jam when it struggled to pass a car parked on a bend. As we headed towards town, we could hear music. And drums. Turning the corner, my cheekbones began to tingle and I became all emotional, being a sucker for a parade, local tradition and a marching band. Corfu is famous for its bands and we were treated to two walking right by us as we made our way to the old town. Flutes, drums, cymbals, saxophones, trumpets and xylophones. A sousaphone player dropped his music so I picked it up from the warm tarmac.

'Hey, Spiros,' the player behind him said, tapping him on the shoulder and pointing to his mislaid sheets.

Of course he was called Spiros. It was the name of the island's patron saint, after all.

On the Liston, I asked a lady if I could take a photo of her palm crosses. She quite happily posed for a picture and then insisted I should have one of the crosses.

'It will help you,' she said.

The Liston filled up with people, the flags were flying and even the dogs were dressed up. And then old St Spyridon himself came by, looking a bit cramped in his silver and gold casket and separated from his hand (in another casket) by several metres and hundreds of years. He was flanked by priests of all shapes and sizes, soldiers in shades carrying guns and an assortment of very important people behind. There was a priest with dyed black hair, goatee and sunglasses, looking for all the world like Peter Sellers; jolly priests with well-trimmed hair and beards and colourful robes; one who was filming the parade as he walked in it and another with a camera over his shoulder, a gift bag in his hand and a ready smile. Bells throughout the old town clanged as the procession walked by, accompanied by some jaunty music from the band while the holy men swung incense ahead of the revered saint.

And then there was one of those moments frozen in time. Our own village priest in the parade, a man in black, looking very serious and walking alone and holding the best palm 'cross' you ever did see, like the top of a bullwhip, almost a miniature palm tree which probably originated from *our* garden yet he did not know it. He glanced my way. I am not sure if he saw me but, in any case, I defiantly held up the palm cross I was given earlier. I hoped he thought of it as a sign: '*Be nice to this foreigner, this Medea, this barbarian. Yes, she is English and, even worse, a woman. But, all in all, she is all right.*'

And then the parade passed. It was a busy day in Corfu Town on Palm Sunday. And it would be even busier the following weekend for Greek Easter.

Before our first guests arrived, I looked in the mirror and realised I had gone native. I'd managed to sort out my inner turmoil but the vision in the looking glass was as if I'd welcomed an ancient, mythological hag into my Greek home. It was time I had my hair cut. For the previous few months I'd been trying to grow it so that I'd look like Meryl Streep in *Mamma Mia*. I figured it would be easier that way, rather than having a new cut every six months. I thought I could plait it, put it on top of my head like Heidi, anything rather than risk going to a Greek hairdresser who might swipe the lot off in one go.

Before we had left, my English hairdresser, who I'd been going to for the last twenty-four years, had pleaded: 'Let me cut it. You're too old for long hair.'

My daughter said the same. But if Meryl Streep could do it, why not me? Damn it, I was only fifty-one. I wasn't ready to be a pixie cut and highlighted fifty-something. The style suited Judi Dench, it was true. But then she had elfin features. The women with pixie cuts I'd seen looked more like ET.

So, six months into our Greek epic, my hair was growing longer. But it wasn't a good thing. I wouldn't have been surprised for snakes to pop out of my barnet, in a style previously modelled by Medusa. It became brittle and tangled and horrible as, at the same time, Andreas's tresses became long enough to tie up into a pony tail.

'Don't you dare, Dad,' said his youngest when he declared that was intention.

So, as we were going back to Blighty for a week in May, I contacted my hairdresser for an appointment. I wanted it tousled, like Lulu: a rock chick rather than an old broiler.

'Sorry,' she said on the phone. 'I'm going on holiday that week.' Ever since, I had been trying to persuade her and a friend to come over for a visit.

'You'd be more than welcome,' I said. 'Just bring your scissors.'

And then I remembered I had my niece's wedding to attend in a few weeks. And, as usual, I became impatient. So I went out and bought a fine-toothed comb, a pair of barber's scissors and watched a video on YouTube. Just how hard could it be?

This hair cutting lark was easy, addictive. A little bit here, a little bit there, a bit more here and then a bit more there. Soon there was a sink full of hair. I was so confident of my new-found skill, I got Andreas in on the act. He now looked like a schoolboy with a pudding basin cut. I, meanwhile, had an unintentional asymmetric bob which looked perfect if I permanently leant my head to the right. I looked scarily like a blonde version of Laurence Olivier as Richard III.

And, to think, we had visitors arriving in less than a week.

And then we heard the cuckoo. How my hair looked really didn't matter.

The swimming pool was still empty. Despite numerous calls to the maintenance man, nothing had been done since he came in February to drain it. They still had to power wash the pool, paint it and move the pump.

'Well,' an ex-pat said. 'That's the Greeks for you. *Avrio, avrio.*'

They said it knowingly, as if they were in Spain and saying *mañana, mañana*.

'It's an English firm, actually,' I said, getting a little fed up with those who were always so eager to speak disrespectfully of their host country.

I was still spending my mornings writing while Andreas prepared the garden for planting and cooked preserved oranges, a scrumptious, syrupy sweet, the recipe for which had been passed on to him by Yanni Pianni's mother from The Three Brothers. With the wonderful navel oranges – known as *merlin* – in abundance and at only 80 cents a kilo, our kitchen cupboards began to burst under the weight of jars full of them.

'Well, they'll be good for our visitors,' Andreas said. And with lots of people coming to stay in the months ahead, the first three arriving in two days' time, every little helped.

121

May

There was a sense of anticipation in Corfu as we approached Holy Week with our three visitors. The church bells rang twice a day as the devout and those not wanting to risk eternal damnation made their preparations for Easter and piled into the church. In the evening, the *plateia* was alive with people as the congregation mingled with the card players and coffee drinkers, beer imbibers and children, who were now on their school holidays and tearing around on bicycles. There were swallows and swallowtail butterflies, hooting owls, croaking frogs, waking cicadas and a host of magical fireflies flitting around the gardens and lanes, their white, winking lights entrancing anyone who looked at them. The air was heavy with the scent of jasmine and mock orange blossom.

One evening, we ventured into the theatre in Corfu Town, courtesy of Gorgeous George and The Graceful Mrs George. We had learned from our mandolin experience never to turn down an invitation.

'It's some choir or other,' I told my English visitors. So we went, completely open-minded and none-the-wiser, to meet our Greek friends on the theatre steps.

Corfu is probably the most musical island in Greece, with more philharmonic bands than you could shake a drumstick at and more music students than notes on the most demanding song sheet you are ever likely to encounter. So whoever was playing would have been good in our book. And then we saw the poster and realised it was rather more than 'some choir or other'.

Greece's finest classical musicians began the programme with what many call the saddest music ever written, Samuel Barber's *Adagio for Strings*. In the auditorium, we were melting in the heat, which came in great waves in between bursts of cool from the air conditioning. We were also melting with the emotion of the music, a wonderful mixture of pathos and passion, a lament in the minor key.

'They played this at my cousin's funeral last week,' one of our visitors whispered, as a tear rolled down his cheek.

And the music played on while a young child of about six in the seat in front of me waved his arms in harmony with the conductor. And then, after the interval, Faure's *Requiem* was performed by the Corfu Municipal Choir. Instruments are beautiful things, and the most beautiful of all is the human voice. With a large choir, the effect on an individual is enormous. It stirs the soul, it takes you to the very heart of the human condition.

And at the end of it, we were all lost for words.

On Good Friday, or Great Friday as the Greeks calls it, we were sitting outside the *kafenio* in the sun before heading to Dukas for our favourite salty roast pork and potatoes. Our guests gave it the thumbs up and we had a ringside seat as the church bells started to ring and the villagers walked by and filled up the *plateia*. With the ladies, I left the table and headed for the back door of the church where Ilia handed out long brown candles with plastic shields to catch the drips. The church was fuller than I had ever seen it.

At the front, the priest conducted a ritual over a 'coffin', covered in red and white carnations and occasional heads of pelargonium. The service finished and the coffin was carried out of the north door and processed solemnly through the main street in the dusk, up a side alley and through the Theotokis church – in one door and out the other – and on to the cemetery church and out through the other side, followed by a host of villagers and their candles. As darkness fell on the village, mothers, fathers and children took their lit candles out into the churchyard and visited the graves of their loved ones. There were glows of orange dotted around the churchyard as the night went on.

This was the ritual of the *ephitafios*, replicated in towns and villages across Greece. It is the most solemn and holy of days, marking the day on which Christ was crucified. Only the knowledge of the resurrection to come and the joy of Easter

123

could pull a believer through it. It was the most spiritual and moving of rituals. The Greek Orthodox religion plays such a big part in village life in Corfu. It is the glue that bonds communities together.

The police were stopping cars going any further than the turning to the market. We parked for free in a car park and headed on foot along the seafront towards the Spilia and the old town. From the windows above the shops, the sound of musicians practising and preparing for a parade wafted out and filled the alleys. At the Liston, a great crowd of people waited for the procession. The parade began. Brass bands, a choir and a heavenly host of priests passed by in the heat, with pride of place going to the casket containing St Spyridon, his crumpled face looking out of the glass in a permanent gaze which looked as if he was crying out. People lined the streets as the parade passed along the Spianada and down towards the sea. Cameras were held high and people craned their necks to get a better look.

The solemnity of the parade passed and the pavements around the top end of the Liston became busier and busier. A great roar from the crowd announced that something was about to happen. In windows up and down the ancient, crumbling buildings, painted pots ranging from great amphorae to small terracotta jugs on sale all through the preceding week appeared from nowhere. Up on the roof of the Arcadion Hotel, a huge red pot the size of a large child was positioned and ready for launch. In a window below, an even larger blue pot was hauled up onto a rail while three men whipped up the crowd and counted down – *trea, dio, ena* – and the pot was released, smashing onto the road below, covering it in broken terracotta and water. The craziness continued for a good half hour, the pots getting bigger and heavier until one almost as big as our village smashed to the floor. And then all hell broke loose, with the crowd surging forward in a desperate attempt to pick up some of the broken pieces and take them home for luck. And our visitors and I dived in too, pulling out seven good bits of decorated terracotta which I would place on the mantelpiece as my offering to Hestia, the goddess of the home and hearth. For

124

days afterwards, the red dust of shattered pottery was scattered through the town's streets and pavements.

When I asked locals what the pot smashing was about, all I got was a shrug of the shoulders.

'It is for Easter,' they said.

'Yes, but why smash pots?' I said.

No-one had a clue.

I was told variously that the pot smashing was a leftover of a pagan tradition reminding Persephone to wake up and come out of Hades to let the Spring begin; or it was a representation of the stoning of Judas Iscariot; or it was the breaking of Christ's tomb; or it was an adaptation of a custom started by the Venetians who threw old things from their bedroom windows on New Year's Day so that they could replace them with new ones.

It was quite possibly a combination of tradition both pagan and Christian. My own view after six months here was that Corfiots just had a liking for making as much noise as possible.

In the evening, the bars of Corfu Town filled up by nine o'clock. In anticipation of what was to come, candle sellers plied their wares – large white candles and plastic cup shields in red, green and blue. A band or two marched through the narrow streets, crashing cymbals and bashing on xylophones. There was a sense of something big about to happen and it filled the warm, evening air.

For years, Yanni Pianni, our friend from The Three Brothers, had been telling us to visit Corfu at Easter.

'You will not believe it. The Greeks are famous for Easter but in Corfu, it is the best.'

And it is true. Words cannot describe the spectacle of that Easter weekend. A strange mixture of ritual, devotion, celebration, tradition, noise, ceremony, moving music, masses of eating and fireworks which, when combined, created a heady experience on a massive scale, with some poignant moments of detail in between.

On the evening of Easter Saturday, we stood with the crowds around the bandstand, a candlelit vigil waiting for the moment of Easter Sunday to arrive and a service relayed by loudspeaker from the church of St Spyridon. The paths to the bandstand became rivers of light. At midnight, there was a great fanfare of crashing band music, choral voices and great rockets and firecrackers in the sky. And then afterwards, the great fast had been broken and it was time for the eating to begin. Tavernas in the town had been booked up in advance for weeks, offering the traditional menu featuring *mayiritsa* soup which consists of rather too many bits of the inside of sheep for my liking. The town buzzed on, well into the early hours.

Up and down the island on Easter Sunday, people feasted with their families on spit-roasted lamb and played smashing games with red-painted, hard-boiled eggs. Rather like in the game of conkers, the winner was the one whose egg remained unbroken when hit by another. We sat on Lambis's terrace, twenty-four of us, enjoying home-reared lamb and goat, local wine, goat's cheese and a cheesecake made by Spiros Bear which was as big as a door. It didn't matter that we had three friends to stay.

'You must bring them,' our host insisted. 'You are all most welcome.'

And he *meant* it.

The ancient concept of *philoxenia* – kindness to strangers – is a unique feature of Greek life. In *The Odyssey*, Penelope counts the cost of it when she is forced to allow the lazy suitors to eat her out of house and home. She has no choice because *philoxenia* is just what you did. The modern Greeks we encountered didn't have very much but their generosity and warmth of spirit never failed to astonish us. And as we sat on Easter Day overlooking the hills and valleys of Corfu with these lovely people, drinking their wine, eating their cheese, we thought to ourselves, *this is something very special.*

And then the tables were turned when we were able to introduce something from home into the mix. Armed with small, chocolate eggs we had brought with us, we descended the steps from the terrace to conceal the spoils all over the garden. Our Easter egg hunt for Betty and Antoni's two children turned out to be something of a novelty. They had never done one before. But their joy in finding the chocolate eggs hidden in their great-uncle's garden was more than matched by ours when they promptly hid them all again for us to find, before brother and sister then alternated between hiding and finding. Their pleasure was in the game rather than the chocolate.

We began to smash the eggs, the victor being Spiros Bear's girlfriend, Natalia, whose strength almost matched his. And then it was time to dive into puddings – a giant cheesecake, a tiramisu and carrot cake, and a huge gateau from Emeral, the popular cake shop on the main road into Corfu Town.

Full of food and wine, we wobbled back home through the olive groves.

As one of our visitors and I emerged from our front door on Easter Monday to the sound of the church bell ringing in the *plateia*, we were joined by Spiros Bear, who had abandoned his bright T-shirt and bandana and was smarter than we had ever seen him, with pressed shirt, dark jeans and polished shoes, his dark, crinkly hair newly-washed, shining and flowing. I couldn't understand it. Spiros in church? That couldn't be right. He had told me church was a place where people went to show off their clothes. And here he was, looking as if he had stepped out from a shop window display.

A crowd of people gathered around the icon of the Virgin and Child, which was draped in red velvet and pinned with gold necklaces, bracelets and earrings and carried by four young men in the *plateia*. A mortar went off unexpectedly and then our own Spiros Bear took centre stage. In an instant, like an expert weightlifter, he hoisted a twenty-foot tall standard from the paving slabs to an upright position. When the congregation had come out of the church, he led the parade along the road past our house and up the winding lane to the church at the top of the village. Along the way, loud bangs cracked through the valley and beyond as mortars were let off by Lovejoy, a local builder.

At the church, the standard was placed along with other smaller ones up against the tower. There was another long service with candles in the church and then the bells rang and it was all over, Spiros having returned just in time to take the pole back down to the *plateia*.

After Easter, we flew back to the UK with our guests for a family wedding and to buy Spiros Waiter a bottle of Giorgio Armani aftershave. May is one of the loveliest months anywhere. In England I always considered it the best month, with wallflowers, tulips and bluebells in abundance. It was a glorious wedding at Richmond, with my niece marrying her military bandsman in a lovely little church with box pews, reclining ruff-collared effigies next to the altar and a Methodist-style gallery where one of the groom's colleagues played a flawless *Trumpet Voluntary*. The rousing hymns – 'Lord of all hopefulness', 'Dear Lord and Father of mankind' and 'Guide me, o Thou great Redeemer' – and the recessional organ music of William Walton's *Crown Imperial* were British to the core and all the more wonderful for it.

Earlier, as the relatives shuffled in after a quick stop at the famous Petersham Nurseries, they gazed around in wonder at the church's quirky interior. There were garlands of flowers and leaves above us, as the bride and groom came into church side by side – a Georgian tradition, the priest said, and reminiscent of a scene from Jane Austen.

Number One Granddaughter followed, a small blonde vision in a wispy aquamarine dress, holding hands with the matron of honour. It was some feat as, at seven years old, she had no inclination to wear a dress at all and would have been much happier wearing the Darth Vader outfit she had been given as a thank you present.

So the bride reached a compromise and fashioned a Jedi lightsaber in white chrysanthemums sprayed light blue. Later, a wedding guest recounted the Georgian tradition of the bride and groom entering the church together, and also, not realising the significance of the 'bouquet', talked confidently about the little bridesmaid carrying a 'hollyhock pole' - *just like in Pride and Prejudice*.

The force was indeed strong with this one.

From the church we walked up across Richmond Park, turning round to gaze at the bridal party against a backdrop of the vast plain of Surrey and the Thames Valley, with lots of green trees, dotted with clusters of houses and a few tower blocks and then an aeroplane flying by. For us country folk, more used to the landscapes of Dorset and Somerset, and some from *oop north*, it was a scene to behold, both ancient and modern.

We strolled by the *Reasons to be Cheerful* bench, installed in Poet's Corner in memory of that great pop music poet, Ian Dury, and then up to Pembroke Lodge, the former home of the Russell family. What a glorious spot. As the children played in some rare sunshine among the trees, this England, surrounded by family, seemed very real and special to a couple of temporary ex-patriots like us. And then the reception with its simple floral arrangements in jam jars and milk bottles, and book cover place settings. As Pop Larkin would have said: *perfick*.

In the evening, the granddaughter turned into Darth Vader and took her turn on the dance floor along with small children breakdancing and sliding across from one side to the other on their knees in traditional style. There was nothing quite like a family wedding.

In West Dorset, there is a view from the A35 road, as it sweeps up over Askers, to reveal one of the most beautiful views of all. After looking to the left and the sweep of the Jurassic Coast, the corner of your right eye is drawn to Eggardon and the lush hinterland, with Pilsdon and Lewesdon– the twin peaks known to sailors as the Cow and Calf – Coney's Castle and Lambert's Castle acting like pulsating echoes in the distance. And the electricity pylons march like giants through Narnia, giving perspective to a landscape so dear to me I almost cried. I thought I was over it, this pull of the land as the native returns. And then we wound our way back to our Dorset *Brigadoon* village in Jack and the Beanstalk land, twixt Cow and Calf.

It was overcast, but the flowers were out on Bluebell Hill. And the sheep grazing in the churchyard had escaped onto the village green. A large and skittish ewe eyed up the play fort before the farmer arrived to round them up. Two circuits of the village later, with cars stopped and residents lending a hand, the sheep were back where they belonged: the churchyard, where they were making a jolly good job of keeping the grass down. The farmer waved at us through the tell-tale hole in the hedge,

129

the signs of *sheepness* right there on the wire. They couldn't wriggle out of this one. Their wool was there for all to see.

So the local accountant fashioned a barrier out of a nearby diversion sign and placed it in the hole until repairs could be carried out. The sheep looked at us, disgusted, before going back to their nibbling.

In villages around the globe, there is never a dull moment.

'Do you like it out there, then?' the farmer asked me from behind the churchyard railings, as if he was talking about us standing in the road rather than about our decision to jack Dorset in for a big fat Greek gap year.

We told him that we did indeed like being in Corfu, although I admitted I'd been homesick.

'Well, I've been around the world a bit,' he said, sagely, recalling his National Service and a trip to Australia to see his wife's brother. 'But I don't think you can beat it here.'

I had to admit that however beautiful Corfu was, there was no place like home.

My brother and sisters, my parents, my children, step-children, grandchildren. I was from a big family and, back in Greece, I missed them all. I missed friends too but, more than anything, I missed the place. It was with a heavy heart that I boarded the early morning plane for Corfu, brought forward to avoid getting tangled up in a strike by Greek air traffic control. And then we were back, back in the sunshine of our Greek village to a chorus of *kalimera*, welcoming smiles and an amaryllis in full bloom on our terrace. There was Spiros the Bear, Spiros Waiter calling at our door to pick up the Timberland boots we had brought him from England, and Paleo Spiros stopping off for an ouzo with us in the *plateia* before going into the *kafenio* for cigarettes.

A whole host of villagers welcomed us back with open arms and phone calls: 'Is everything all right? Have you had a good time?'

Yes, we had, but it was also good to be back. There were still so many mixed emotions.

It was a wonderful time of year to be on the island but many of the resorts were still very quiet. It was early days, but hardly a day went by without a cruise ship or two in the port.

The air was warm and full of red dust. From our terrace, we could hear the sounds of village life: clapping at the primary school playground as the teacher shouted out instructions to her young charges, children singing, a motorbike buzzing by and a hubbub of voices in the garden next door as our neighbours inspected their vegetables for ants.

In the mornings the aroma of bubbling moussaka and *pastitsada* wafted across to the Villa Oleander from Elizabeth's Taverna. A cockerel crowed, sparrows chirruped, bright yellow butterflies fluttered by and then a swallow did a body swerve as it landed on our washing line. It checked the progress of its mate which was attempting to build a nest above one of our windows. Throughout the village, there were swallows, swifts and house martins by the dozen, chattering, laughing, zooming and hardly ever stopping. And in the square, they dive-bombed the village cat, the bug-eyed cat that had been at death's door a month or so ago until a kind English lady spent a fortnight giving it medicine from the vet and paying to have it spayed.

Stray cats could be a nuisance here, feral and unloved, although their presence at the bins kept the rodents down. The Greeks as a nation don't treat domestic animals very well. They are considered a hindrance, an annoyance – something far removed from the English way of doing things. Stray dogs are commonplace and every house or patch of land seems to have a dog chained up outside, keeping watch but desperate for company.

Now, after her treatment, the village cat was as right as rain. At the last count, she had killed three swallows.

'She goes in to have surgery,' said Kiki at the *kafenio*, 'and she comes out a killer. She is Terminator.'

Survival of the fittest.

Our year here was about to change. We prepared ourselves for the months ahead, when the weeks on our calendar would be almost back-to-back with visits from family and friends. Our house, which we'd had to ourselves all winter, would be a microcosm of the island itself. From now until mid-August, there would be sheets to wash and dry, bathrooms to clean, beds to make and airport runs there and back. A total of twenty-six guests during our gap year, and most of them during the summer season. It was great to see people. But it was a lot of housework. And for a writer whose routine had been to be at her desk by eighty-thirty each morning, self-discipline would have to be even more rigorously applied. I was working, our visitors were not. But, just as Corfu's visitors were good for the island, so our visitors would be good for us.

On 21 May, there were big parades through Corfu Town to mark the ceding of the seven Ionian Islands from the British protectorate to Greece in 1864. The Corfiots were always having parades for one thing or another and it was difficult to keep track of what was what. Bands, children in costume, a huge Greek flag, and musicians playing the theme music to *The Great Escape* and 'Life on the Ocean Wave.'

He was some distance away and it was Andreas who saw him first. Our village priest, walking alongside a group of children with special needs. Without a thought, my husband waved to him. The priest waved back and came up to Andreas and shook his hand, before squinting over his spectacles and realising who it was. But it was too late by then, the spell had been broken. Reparation had occurred, our differences put behind us as we joined in with the Corfiots in celebration of being given back to Greece.

Part IV

Summer

'Gradually, the magic of the island settled over us as gently and clingingly as pollen.'

Gerald Durrell, *My Family and Other Animals*

June

A high wind whipped through the trees as the children prepared for the end of term show.

The stage, which had a backdrop depicting the rocky outcrop of the Athenian Acropolis and the Parthenon, was set up outside on the gravelled playground. Mothers and fathers, aunties, uncles and grandparents huddled around tables, waiting for the concert to begin.

A group of enthusiastic six-year-olds entered stage left, the boys dressed as ancient Greek soldiers and the girls in classical-style, white dresses, each with one shoulder bared. The reluctant few, and there weren't many with stage fright, were egged on by their glamorous teacher in heels as high as the mountain that overlooked the village. The children acted, they danced and they sang as the women went on strike and withdrew their labour as a protest at their husbands being away at war. With Greek music, extracts from the sassy and laid-back theme tune to *The Pink Panther* and a disco power ballad, Gloria Gaynor's 'I Will Survive', the girls took the higher moral ground and refused to co-operate unless their menfolk came home. It was a classic tale of gender wars, based on *Lysistrata* by Aristophanes, first performed in 411 BC and a comic account of one woman's determination to end the Peloponnesian War.

It was clear that the children did not know too much about the strike (which was probably just as well, because it's all about withdrawing sexual favours) but they performed their version of the play with aplomb and great joy. Their marathon effort was followed by short performances by older classes and ended in a spirited rendition of the hokey cokey in Greek. And then the games began, with the children high on the wind and cans of Coke being dispensed by one of the parents from a fridge in the corner of the playground. The mums and dads drank beer and looked forward to a *souvlaki* a bit later on as the smoke rose from the grill. The children ran in lines to retrieve marshmallows

135

buried in two cream cakes and then danced to 'Gangnam Style' as the PE teacher prepared for musical chairs. And when the victor was declared, his dancing classmates ran to him, crowded around and raised him aloft as if he'd just won the Olympic Games. I had never seen children quite as caring as this.

They were excited, happy and full of good spirit, especially to each other. It was hardly surprising as they were now on holiday for ten whole weeks. An endless summer stretching out before them. As we headed home at just after eight o'clock, the fun continued well into the night, the last ones winding their way back at one in the morning.

Dark red, pink and white hollyhocks lined the roadsides and, in the garden, the vegetables were growing faster than we could water them. The writing routine I had imposed upon myself at the outset was beginning to pay off. My novella based on my blog was available on Kindle and was about to be published as a paperback. I had secured a bit of feature writing with a magazine, which made me feel better about myself because I was at least contributing something to the household budget.

It was getting hotter in Corfu now, with temperatures soaring. The seventies tabloid moniker *'Cor-phew'* was right on the button. Swallows and swifts dived into the water, the cicadas' chirruping chorus was deafening and the white tourists from the cruise ships who wandered around Corfu Town were getting redder and were covered in mosquito bites.

With my best friend staying with us from Dorset, it was time to dive into the grounds of Mon Repos, the birthplace of the Duke of Edinburgh on the edge of the island's ancient capital, Paleopolis. It was a shady spot, with plenty of cover. The mansion itself, which was built in 1830 in the neoclassical style, could do with some tender, loving care. And the museum inside is a bit of a mish-mash, with the age of exhibits spanning thousands of years. The Brits and American visitors probably wonder why Prince Philip hardly gets a mention, with the building playing host to various exhibitions, none of which relate to HRH. But the prince was only eighteen months old when the Greek royal family was exiled on 3 December 1922. Hardly time to get to know the place.

Despite its run-down appearance and haphazard displays, or maybe *because* of them, I liked Mon Repos. It seemed home-spun and unpretentious. With the island's archaeological museum closed until 2015 for renovation (I'd been dying to get back there and see Medusa again), I had been missing my ancient artefacts fix; so to find a room stacked full of ancient *stelae* was, for me, as good as finding a new shoe shop. I'm quite happy to spend all day in dusty museums stacked with grave markers, votive goods, bits of ancient jewellery, arrowheads and figures of Artemis. Although on that day in Mon Repos, it was hot and stuffy and the air conditioning didn't seem to be on. So we walked out through the imposing front door and took a walk around the grounds where a cool breeze rustled through the leaves of the trees. We pushed on, heading for a ruined temple I knew to be here somewhere. Mon Repos was built on the site of Paleopolis, the ancient town of Kerkyra, and several interesting things had been found in the grounds and beyond its walls. The Medusa pediment itself came from the Temple of Artemis, the ruins of which are not far from the entrance to Mon Repos.

'Are you sure it's here?' my husband said, weary now and just wanting a beer.

'Yes, it's got to be here somewhere,' I said. 'I've seen pictures of it. I think there are at least two of them.'

Just as we were about to turn back, we saw some large pieces of cut stone lying on the ground, with three young people doing some sort of archaeological dig. It spread over a wide area. This, I read later, was thought to be the temple of Hera, which dated back to before the seventh century BC. There was another one somewhere, the temple of Poseidon, but we never found it. We strolled on and came to the remains of a Doric temple, thought to be dedicated to Apollo. The ruin was just old stones now with a few upright columns. But, if you thought hard enough, you could imagine it in all its glory, looking out to sea before the trees had grown so high and obscured the view.

'There's a path there,' my husband said, pointing to a gap in the trees.

'Do you think…?'

'What?' my friend said. 'What do you think?'

Andreas and I looked at each other.

'Are you going to tell her or am I?'

'No,' I said. 'You do it. You tell a much better tale than me.'

So he proceeded to tell my friend about our search for the Kardaki Spring. To us, the spring had been as elusive as Will o' the Wisp. Every time we were close, paths led to dead ends. The sun would beat down and we'd be thwarted by the heat or by brambles, like a prince and princess in a fairytale by the Brothers Grimm.

'It's said that whoever drinks from the spring is destined to forget their homeland and always return to Corfu,' I said, butting in.

'Well,' my friend said. 'I'm not sure you should be drinking from it then.'

She was happy to visit us for a week but wanted us back in Dorset.

'Once your year is over, you'll get it out of your system,' she had said, admitting that she missed us.

But however homesick I had felt, Corfu had now got under our skin. It had burrowed, like a larva, until it was well established and ready to meet the world as a new bug. As we drank the wine, soaked up the olive oil with bread, it had entered our veins and become a part of us.

Now was as good a time as any to find the Kardaki Spring.

So we clambered on along the narrow path and over a wall before joining what looked to be the proper path with steps down to the sea. Down we went and there, in a wall, was that symbol of Venice we had seen all over the old parts of Corfu Town: a winged lion, the lion of St Mark, nestled into the wall, surrounded by green ferns and with a spout of clear water coming from its mouth. It was cool to the touch, and quenched our thirsts.

'You've done it now,' I said to my friend. 'That means you'll have to come back too.'

So we went down from the spring to the small beach where we watched a group of young Greek boys jumping from a jetty as we pondered our fate.

There was a shout from next door.

'Hey!' the gruff voice said. 'What you doing?'

It was Spiros Bear's usual greeting, as he walked in through the gate accompanied by a small bundle of beige hair on little legs.

'What's that?' I said.

'I have new puppy.'

'What is it?' It looked like a small version of Chewbacca, the Wookie in the film *Star Wars*.

'He is *griffon canis*,' Spiros said. 'He is my daughter's. We get boy this time. We no want puppies.'

This small shaggy creature moved in tune with Spiros. He was only eight weeks old but already playfully devoted to his new master.

'What's his name?'

'We don't know. Maybe we call him *Maimou*.'

'What does that mean?'

'It is Greek for monkey.'

It seemed appropriate. Everywhere the organ grinder went, the *maimou* went too.

When you are writing for a magazine, it can take you to all sorts of places and bring you into contact with all sorts of people. I had first come across Jan Manessi on the Corfu Grapevine, a Facebook group for people living on the island, many of whom were ex-pats. Jan always spoke such sense online and with a knowledge of the island and its culture I envied. When she was verbally abused by a racist Brit who would frequently set the hares running by making a statement about the world being overtaken by immigrants – the irony of him living in Corfu seemed to have passed him by – I wanted to hug her there and then, even though I'd never met her. I could see from the racist's Facebook profile that he was a supporter of the BNP and had boasted on his wall about the fun he was having stirring up the folk on Corfu Grapevine.

So I contacted Jan to offer her my support and asked if I could do an interview with her for the magazine for which I was writing. I met her on the main road just before Benitses and she drove me up the track to the St Stefanos mansion, one of those beautiful Venetian mansions dotted all over Corfu.

Built in 1782 with a view to the sea and across the Corfu Channel, it's an impressive, solid and dramatic old house clinging to a rock with its own church and olive groves.

The house has been beautifully restored, retaining character features which are complemented by antique furniture, family portraits and sumptuous colours on the walls and a light and airy interior.

Its visitors' book reads like an international list of VIPs. Signatures of the author and naturalist Gerald Durrell, who had done so much to raise the profile of the island; Kaiser Wilhelm II, who used to like to watch the sunset up at Pelekas; the entire Greek royal family in 1900; Cecil Lewis, who co-founded the BBC; the actress Vivien Leigh; American art collector and socialite Peggy Guggenheim. And so the list goes on.

These days, visitors come from all walks of life because Jan lets out the five-bedroomed Palladian-style mansion and stays with friends when the holidaymakers arrive.

Her connection with the island began in the 1960s when she visited it as a holidaymaker.

'In the 1970s I came to work for Olympic Holidays,' she told me as we sat out on the balcony. 'I had been working in Kenya for a theatre company. I went back to London and walked back into the office and decided I wanted to do something that involved travel.'

So she came to Corfu. But before she arrived, friends asked if she would look in on their aunt on the island who had broken her leg.

'That's when I met my future husband, Stephen, who was visiting the lady at the same time as me.'

They were married eighteen months later, in 1976, and went on to have two sons.

When she first saw the house, Jan was completely bowled over by the view. She loved the way of life there.

She continued working in the holiday business as a rep, spending her time between Corfu and Oxford, where her sons went to school. She worked in social housing as an estate manager until April 2011. Sadly her husband, Stephen Manessis, died in 2003.

San Stefano, which was completed in 1782 after an earthquake destroyed the previous house, came into the Manessis family in the early 20th century as Stephen's mother's dowry. She was from the noble Flamburiari family and the house had been built by one of her forebears. It has been restored twice, once twenty years ago and the second time in 2009.

'When I came here there was only cold water in the kitchen and there was only one bathroom,' Jan said.

The San Stefanos estate features in *Corfu: The Garden Isle*, the beautiful book given to me by Kiki about mansions of Corfu. There are mansions like these all over Corfu, some of them inhabited but many of them crumbling. They are a remnant of the island's past when the Venetian nobility were in charge.

I had first met Maria Strani-Potts back home in the UK when she and her husband, Jim, had put together an anthology of prose, poetry and photographs in a book called *Dorset Voices*. She lived close to me in Dorchester but spent much of her time in Greece, having been born in Corfu. Her novel, *The Cat of Portovecchio: Corfu Tales*, is a fascinating, literary glimpse into how Greek village life used to be.

Her short story, 'The Pimping of Panorea', is a modern-day fable of what can happen to a beautiful place when development goes unchecked.

When I last spoke to Maria, she had real hopes and fears for her native land, which she continues to visit with Jim, a former director of the British Council. She has fond memories of growing up on the island in the 1950s. She was born the daughter of intellectual parents, not far from the Cavalieri Hotel, and childhood socialising took place by the sea.

'I remember summer nights playing with my friends in the *Pano Plateia* until late at night. The scent of jasmine, lemon, orange and lime blossom, as well as various sea smells, are still with me.'

She said: 'Now, I feel like a political dissident. My feelings towards Greece are mixed and often angry. We love Greece, and it hurts to see the way it is at the moment.'

Maria thinks the Ionian Islands must start producing their own food again.

'They need to re-invent agriculture. We have the best climate in the world and yet we grow next-to-nothing. Our milk, meat, lemons, oranges, all products that thrive in our climate, are largely brought in from outside. We have destroyed most of our fish stock. We continue to destroy it through fish farming and chemical interventions.

'Tourism is a good, clean, easy economy but unless, like everything else, it is planned responsibly and meticulously, it will continue to be a monster and a culturally destructive element in our lives.'

Up in our village, it seemed that everyone had their own plot of land where they grew something. Olive trees were maintained and the trimmings used for winter fires. The olives were harvested and turned into oil, as we had seen at Vistonas. Our own friends had their own goats, hens, turkeys and verdant vegetable plots. Surplus fruit and vegetables were shared with others or turned into sauces, dried or frozen. It seemed that many of our Greek friends were almost self-sufficient and were turning more and more to their land to get them through the dark days of austerity. But it was true, there were orange and lemon trees growing fruit at the drop of a hat yet they were never harvested. And the supermarket greengrocery shelves were stocked with things that had never ever touched Ionian soil. As with elsewhere, it was clear that many people still needed to reconnect with the food they ate by nurturing the raw material to a point where they could cook and eat it. But the supermarket lifestyle is convenient, easy, in all countries of the world. But Maria was right. Local produce had to be better, environmentally, nutritionally and economically. What we couldn't grow in our own garden or be given by our neighbours, we would buy in the market, with our friend Eleni thrusting under our noses her latest 'Corfu speciale', which varied according to the season. It was the best way to shop.

By mid-June, the pool was finally up and running, its maintenance taken over by someone much more reliable. Pete the Pool came twice a week to keep it clean and tidy, a service included in the rent for the summer. A pool had not been on our wish list but during the hot summer months it was a godsend. Our visitors would have hours of fun and Ilia and Koula's daughter-in-law Betty would come around regularly so that Little Ilias and Marie Angela could cool off.

Betty and I would sit and talk by the pool and have a cup of tea while my husband turned his melons so they would get an even burst of sunshine.

'I am so pleased you came to the village,' she said. 'You are my friends, you are part of our family.'

I had chilled out so much now that I was no longer rigid when someone tried to hug me, which Betty did frequently.

Betty worked too many hours at a local taverna for not much money. It was hard for her, hard for young mothers on a holiday island in a time of financial crisis, when the only work they could find was seasonal. They were at their busiest just when their children had broken up from school for the long summer holidays.

To celebrate the publication of my novella, we went for a meal at Elizabeth's. There in the corner was Yannis of the Mohican and White Sunglasses partaking quietly of his daily evening meal. When we had finished, he came over to join us.

'It is okay if I sit with you?' he said.

Of course it was. We were always keen for a bit of local flavour. The excellent home-made wine flowed and so did the conversation. Yannis told us some of the best local places to take our visitors – the swimming pools, bars and tavernas. He taught us some Greek words and became very excited when I told him my surname.

'Grigg – it means Greek!' he said. 'You are Greek.'

I have looked it up since and, of course, it doesn't. But by the second litre of wine I told him I had always suspected as much. I wrote down phrases in my notebook, the writing getting bigger and more illegible.

I was fine until I went out of the door. And then I collapsed in the evening air into Andreas's arms. The next morning, my earrings, which had been in a pot on my dressing table, were all over the bedroom floor and blood was smeared all over the bathroom tiles.

'What the hell happened?' I said, staring at the mess.

'You fell into the dressing table, stubbed your toe and then I had to undress you and put you to bed.'

'Well, thanks very much,' I said. 'You could have stopped me from drinking so much.'

'It's okay,' he said. 'I drank too much too.' But, as usual, he was none the worse for it. I think I had only seen him with a hangover twice in the fifteen years we had been together.

And then we laughed. We had set out to be non-typical Brits. We wanted to fit into a Greek way of life, meet local people and not become known for our drinking excesses. With a bit of luck, Yannis and his family had forgotten all about it.

'How's your head?' Yannis said, his scooter propped up next to the wall of the *kafenio* later that day. 'My daughter was so worried for you, she was going to order a taxi home.'

Taxi home? We only lived one hundred yards away from the taverna.

I looked across at Andreas.

'Oh dear,' I said.

'Oh dear, indeed,' he said. He and Yannis exchanged sniggers and ordered an ouzo. I stuck with lemonade.

July

Up at the *plateia*, the mandolins did a sound check to 'Zorba's Dance.' Children tore around the square's twin trees and toddlers bobbed up and down on bended knees while devoted mothers and grannies looked on. Old men sat outside the *kafenio*, clacking their worry beads, gazing out at the scene unfolding before them.

The butcher arrived in his van with two crates of *souvlakia* as the barbecue to the side of the *kafenio* began to smoke. Wine, beer and Coca Cola flowed; and plates and plates of *souvlakia*, oily roast potatoes with aubergines, chicken and peppers kept arriving on our table, courtesy of Nikos, the accountant, even though we hadn't ordered it.

'You want more wine? I bring you more wine,' he said and wandered down the road to his house to bring back a fancy decanter of his home-made brew, his own feta and green olives.

'Why do they keep giving us all this?' said our two grown-up children, who were staying with us for the week.

We weren't sure.

I stopped Kiki as she came out to pick up some glasses from the tables.

'Don't worry,' she said. 'It is like a present to you from Nikos. He is the village president, he *wants* you to have it.'

The village president? The loud card player with a different tracksuit for each day of the week? We had been accepted. It felt good.

The women danced in lines, around and around the trees, and were joined by the men. The song and the tempo changed and a slim, middle-aged holidaymaker emerged from the sidelines to stun everyone with her energetic Turkish-style shimmy, dirty dancing with a man called Nikos from Gardelades, who produced T-shirt after T-shirt from his backpack all through the night. A chair overturned and a man fell out of it, hitting his head on the paving slabs. There were

145

momentary looks of concern and then laughter when it was clear all was well. Long-haired Kosta took the microphone and began to croon. Kosta Elvis was his name, which seemed most appropriate. This must have been the Elvis we had been told about by an English couple who Spiros Waiter had seated next to us in Dukas one Sunday because 'you are both English; you will have things to talk about' – although it was more to do with the taverna being busy and space being at a premium.

A line of male dancers made their way in and out through the *kafenio* in a conga-style line but with a Greek flavour.

And still the food kept coming.

'You think this is busy! You wait until our *panegyri* in a few weeks' time,' Kiki said.

The next thing we knew, my husband had been pulled up from the table by Nikos the President for the pigeon dance. Several of them moved around in small circles, close to the ground, sizing each other up. And then they all sat round a table, boys together having fun.

About twenty minutes later, my step-daughter said: 'You'll never guess what. Not only has Dad had ouzo and three glasses of wine, he's now on beer and Retsina.'

By the time he came back to our table, Andreas, the president and three other men had polished off a bottle of Jaegermeister. The dancing went on into the night. My son and I propped up Andreas all the way home and he was put into bed in the recovery position.

At Yanni Pianni's the next day, we sat out at our favourite table, the children slumped in the hangover position and Andreas still looking rather green.

'Ah, you have *panegyri* last night, I think,' Yanni said.

'How did you guess?' I said as I ordered our lunch.

'It is always the same,' Yanni said, pulling up a chair. 'You will know the next time.'

At the airport it was time to say goodbye to my son and step-daughter and welcome my son-in-law and granddaughter off the incoming flight. They passed like ships in the night. The airport run was becoming a common occurrence.

Number One Granddaughter strode out to the arrivals hall as if she had been there in a previous life. A new eight-year-old but already with the wisdom of Solomon.

'Hello, Granny,' she said, holding her hand out to give me a high-five. 'When are we going to Aqualand?'

Two days later, and we were there, saving ourselves more than thirty-five euros because we were 'residents'. This water park in the middle of Corfu is widely advertised – on every bus shelter, brochure and lamppost, billed as one of the most amazing and adventurous water parks in Europe. Now I don't know if that's true, having never been to one before so therefore having nothing to compare it with. But getting there as soon as the gates opened and picking our spot, we certainly got our money's worth. The grandchild went down all the chutes she possibly could, over and over again, and was most put out by height restrictions on the scariest rides which meant she couldn't go on them.

'But why can't I do the vertical drop?' she said, inching her way to its steps.

'I don't know,' I said, 'but I'm sure there's a very good reason.'

I'm more of a watcher than a participant. Nearly drowning is not my idea of fun. And I once heard an urban myth in which someone was lacerated by a razor blade inserted in a plastic chute at a similar place in Dorset. The horror of that has been at the forefront of my mind in these situations ever since. To say I'm wary is an understatement. But having the world's most fearless granddaughter and a husband and son-in-law who are very similar, there was no escaping it.

Down the crazy river my husband and I went, safely ensconced in a rubber ring made for two, only for me to get all the G-force because I was in front with a large object (Andreas) behind me and plunging head first into the water at the same spot every time, much to the amusement of passers-by. As a child, I was once rescued from the undertow in a tidal estuary in North Devon by my older sister's friend. I was only about three at the time and can't really remember it but it had obviously lodged in my subconscious. I have had a fear of going underwater ever since I can remember and no cajoling, tricking

147

or reassurance can overcome it. That's just the way I am. So to do what I did at Aqualand took great courage, especially when I would much rather have been sitting in the shallows of the wave pool, a delight not shared by my grandchild.

'This is boring, Granny,' she said. 'Let's go down the Black Hole.'

Down at our local beach of Paleokastritsa, we hired a boat after Spiros Bear introduced us to a friend who would give us the best price. Our neighbour was always very protective, never wanting anyone to take advantage of us. We knew we were blessed to have as our neighbour a Greek guardian angel as kind, strong and knowledgeable as Spiros.

The resort is a busy place in the height of summer, with people packed like sardines on its main beach. But it's possible to get away from it all by packing a picnic and heading off to one of the many lovely beaches accessible only by boat. It was from one of these that my fearless granddaughter learned to snorkel in the cool, clear waters of Paleokastritsa.

'Why don't you do it, Granny?' she said.

I told her I had a phobia about putting my face in the water. I didn't even like the rubber mask around my face and biting on the snorkel mouthpiece. It was a feeling of being trapped, I suppose.

'Wimp,' she said, as she turned her head and flippered her way around the headland with her father.

'Why don't you try it?' Andreas said. 'The fish are just amazing. You'd love it.'

Every time over almost two decades that he had put on a snorkel, he said the same. You would have thought he would have got it by now. To get me on a boat had been a minor miracle. Now he was just pushing it.

So the three of them explored the clear waters while I, bobbing up and down at anchor, prepared lunch. There were a few people on the shore, with hire boats coming and going and a water taxi doing the rounds. We had been told to get back just after lunch because the wind was set to blow up during the afternoon. When it was time to go, the last boiled egg safely tucked away in my granddaughter's stomach, my son-in-law pulled on the anchor to haul it up. But it held fast. Stuck. And too deep to go down safely to get out by hand. For the next twenty minutes, we manoeuvred the boat this way and that in an attempt to free the anchor, which I could see through the rippling water was wedged under a ledge. The wind built up, slowly at first, but it was clear that something was on its way. That's the thing about the Ionian. You think it's calm and easy but, in just a few minutes, the sea state can change as the wind picks up further up the coast and heads your way. When sailing, I had learnt it paid to pay close attention to the shipping forecast, which was always pretty accurate.

'We'd just as well cut the ropes and leave it,' I said. 'We'll just have to pay for a replacement.'

And with that, the boat edged forward, the anchor came loose and we were free. So we pulled up the rope and headed back, hugging the shoreline as the sea began its metamorphosis.

After a week, my granddaughter's visit was over. It had been a wonderful boost to see her and watch as she enjoyed the island to the full. I was sorry I could not have taken her to see Medusa at the archaeological museum, which was closed for refurbishment until 2015. She would have liked that. But probably she liked Aqualand better.

It was a leisurely changeover this time, with a few days in between visitors. I was becoming intimately connected with the sheets and pillowcases I washed and ironed, the floors I mopped and the surfaces I dusted. Our visitors were frequent and welcome, because they had been invited. But it confirmed to me something about myself that I already knew. I could never run a bed and breakfast. The idea of cleaning up after people and being nice to strangers in my own home was anathema.

We were harvesting our first melons, the cherry tomatoes kept on coming, and there was a glut of aubergines, beans, peppers, courgettes, rocket, lettuce and radishes. We picked and froze them, made up batches of ratatouille and were pleased with ourselves for keeping on top of this never-ending supply of fresh vegetables, only to find a bag of vegetables left on our doorstep by others who were also experiencing a glut. Our visits to the market were infrequent now that we were growing our own; but every now and then we would pop in for some fresh fish or seafood and say *kalimera* to Eleni.

To say the ground was fertile was an understatement. To think, when we started out on this journey, our outside space was more like a pastoral nightmare.

'The house before, it was a mystery,' Kiki said. 'All dark and overgrown outside. But now, you have opened it up and let the sun in. Everyone has been commenting. You have done such a good job with the garden.'

They call Corfu The Garden Isle. It was lush and green, even at this time of year when the sun was baking hot and visitors and locals dived into the sea to cool off. Gerald Durrell described it as The Garden of the Gods. You could imagine them strolling around, plucking an apricot from a tree and cavorting with nymphs through the olive groves, a Hellenistic pastoral romance, where everything in the garden was lovely.

But of course, everything in the garden wasn't lovely. Times were hard, politicians were invariably described as 'dirty'. Ordinary people struggled to keep their heads above water. From the news reports, we could see it was in the cities where they felt it most. Here on the island, there were people we knew who were just pleased to have a job even though they were getting far below the minimum wage. In the villages, people cultivated their patches of land and lived a life more simple.

There were long faces outside the *kafenio*. The village *panegyri*, the long-awaited festival to celebrate St Paraskevi, had been called off. With a week's notice, the organisers had been told by the owner of the field where the festival has been held for years: '*Oxi.*' Which, in Greek, means no.

It was a blow for the village, for community life. It was a blow for the organisers, who worked hard to put on these events for the benefit of all. And it was a blow to us, too, as my brother and his family had booked their holiday dates around it.

The reason for the refusal, as conveyed to my husband and me, seemed to hinge on the owner of the field feeling snubbed because he had not been chosen to coach the village football team. There are always two sides to every story. But to say we had been excited about the event was an understatement. We had walked past this field of olive trees for the past ten months. We'd seen the stage and the stacked-up chairs, the light fittings and the ice cream fridge - or was it for beer? We saw the YouTube clip, we heard the stories. How would it compare with our own weekend of fun back in Lush Places? We were ready for the St Paraskevi *Panegyri* and sold it lock, stock and barrel to my brother's family.

Yes, there were other *panegyri*, throughout the summer months. And I knew there were some people who'd lived here for years who were sick and tired with them. But I was only here for a year and wanted all the village culture I could get. And this was *our panegyri*, a chance to see the people we had lived with since October get up and dance, join hands with them, and have a good time on home territory. The saving grace was that there was another *panegyri* in the village later in August. But by then, my brother's family would be gone. So we looked at all the banners and posters on the roadside to see what other festivals would be on while they were with us. There were plenty.

There was a shovel waiting on the upstairs balcony, ready to deal with our latest visitor. It had appeared one night not long after a small white cat turned up mewing in the garden, closely followed by a bat. With Doctor Seuss timing, something that rhymes with *mat* suddenly appeared in the vine overhead.

And it was not a hat.

There it was, looking down on the family gathering on the outside terrace with cold, beady eyes. And then, once we'd spotted it, it shot off, like the proverbial rat up a drainpipe, although it found its way up by shinning up a pillar and on to the roof.

And the next day, it was back. Andreas devised some elaborate way of dispatching the blighter, and to my eternal disappointment, it did not involve getting a kitten.

I named the rat Scabbers, after Ron Weasley's familiar in *Harry Potter*. I believe if I ridiculed it and sort of de-demonised it, the thought of it out there ready to pounce would not make my skin crawl.

151

We had just picked up a vehicle for my big brother from Kostas and Antonis at the appropriately-named Sunrise Car Hire, a place near the port surrounded by sunflowers. They were nice people, giving us good rates. Kostas always came out with something he had grown in his garden. This time it had been fresh figs.

As with anywhere, you had to drive carefully. But when we moved here in October last year, we thought the Corfiot drivers had turned over a new leaf. No tailgating, no overtaking on blind bends and everyone driving much slower than in the summer. Ah, we thought, they were economising, because driving slower uses less petrol.

And then came the summer.

'The drivers are still crazy, y'know,' said Canadian George, a Corfiot who'd spent more than twenty years in Vancouver. 'You have to stay close to the side of the road. It can be dangerous. You don't know what's coming round the corner.'

It could be a dog, a tortoise, a hedgehog, a hare, or a horse on a long tether. But, more likely than not, it would be another car straddling the centre line.

On the day we went to pick up my brother and his family from the airport, we had just pulled up at traffic lights. A car beside us was stopped and in front was a man in a suit on a scooter. Like many others, he was not wearing a crash helmet.

The car's middle-aged passenger, dressed in just shorts and a baseball cap, got out and started slapping the scooter rider around the head. I didn't like to look too closely in case the assailant saw me and pulled out a baseball bat from the boot.

Incredibly, the scooter rider (and we still don't know who was in the wrong or what happened – maybe they were long-lost friends), just shook his head, took the slaps, and smiled before pulling away when the lights turned green.

Taking my brother to our home from the airport later that day, we were tailgated and then overtaken by a driver who promptly gave us the bird. Nice. A few days later, we saw the remains of a minor accident near a major road junction. At almost the same spot five years ago, a lorry had absentmindedly hit my vintage VW Beetle in the bottom while were waiting at traffic lights to get the ferry back home.

'I so sorry, I pay for damage,' the large, pony-tailed driver had said. 'I am in hurry. I have to get to the port. Let me have your address. I am Nakis from Kontokali; everyone knows me.'

Everyone might know him but he never coughed up. If you're reading this and he's sitting next to you, please give him a nudge. In our experience, Corfiots are men and women of their word. Nakis disappointed us.

In the Ropa Valley, we saw a car overturned in a ditch. A group of people were trying to get it back on four wheels. We learned later that the vehicle had suffered a tyre blow-out. Poor driver – but lucky to be alive.

Of course, accidents happen everywhere. Instead of shrines at the side of the road, in the UK we have bouquets to remind us how lives can be wiped out in an instant. I was reminded of an evening some years ago when we were approaching a bend on a drive from Sidari to Kassiopi. We were overtaken by two cars, the drivers playing chicken. About ten minutes later, on the outskirts of Kassiopi, we met a stationary coach with one of the two cars flattened underneath it. The bus passengers were being helped off, dazed and shaken. We pulled to a halt, the road was blocked, the police arrived and so, too, did the lady doctor, who looked glamorous as she pulled on her rubber gloves. And then a wail went up as the mother of the young driver arrived on the scene. He had been killed in an instant.

A year later and we paid our respects at the shrine installed at the spot.

It still gave me chills, just thinking about it. And whenever we drove along that stretch of road, the scenes played out in my head. And when I saw crazy drivers – most of them young men – I would always think there was another one who was far too young to join the ranks of the death notices displayed on telegraph poles. Most of all, I felt sorry for the innocent people they endangered, and their families.

It was never worth it.

Back in the village, we sat down for dinner at Dukas, where my niece and her friend were presented with a rooster *pastitsada* the size of a small village. We gorged on pork from the oven as Spiros Waiter talked about football to my husband. His eyes suddenly alighted on my brother's wrist. He was like a magpie. Shiny, shiny.

'Your watch,' he said. 'It very nice.'

My brother held out his arm.

'Thanks,' he said. 'But it's a fake.'

'How much you want for it?' Spiros Waiter said.

'I don't want anything,' my brother said. 'It's a fake.'

'It is very good fake,' Spiros Waiter said. 'I give you one hundred euros.'

August

In Paleokastritsa, parking was at a premium. We sauntered down to the Apollon restaurant which overlooked the main beach and were shown to our table, which we had been advised to book well in advance. We had family with us and were meeting our friend Gorgeous George and his lovely wife for dinner. It was early yet, the sun still warm in the sky. But already, people were beginning to stake their claim on spots on the beach, with towels, picnic chairs and rugs. In the centre of this pretty crescent-shaped bay, the water slowly rippled around the base of a stage set into the water. Children swam around it while on the shore, sound checks echoed across the bay.

As the darkness fell and the sun went down, an early evening planet illuminating the sky, the road between us and the sea became thronged with people. There were stalls selling candyfloss and cheap-looking toys, popcorn and sweetcorn, with bright white lights strung up over each one. Gypsies walked by with great bunches of garish balloons.

From around the promontory, a red light glided into the cove, accompanied by mandolins and the stirring voices of the Corfu Choir. The boat, complete with rigging, fixed sail and a trail of red smoke, came in slowly towards the shore. Carefully, the captain brought the vessel to the back of the stage and the choristers climbed off, one by one, before assembling in formation. They reeled off Greek song after song, including 'Kerkyra', which we had first heard at the mandolin concert before Easter. Their repertoire over, the choir said farewell, climbed back on their boat and sailed off, singing, around the headland. Then it was time for the members of the dance troupe from Krini, a village up in the hills between Paleokastritsa and Angelokastro, to cavort around the stage in traditional costume. They danced the way only Greeks can, with energy, elegance and great joy.

There was a short lull, with the sounds of people – invisible now in the darkness but packed like sardines on the beach – chattering in Greek, English, German and Italian. Gorgeous George and his wife got up to stretch their legs and explore the busy street. When they came back they told us they had bumped into the Mayor of Corfu, an old friend, and they agreed with him that the evening was already turning into something quite special.

And then it came.

A flash lit up the bay as a group of small boats, bearing red lights and trailing smoke, came closer, their crimson reflections on the water flowing outwards in ever-increasing circles. They were led by a large rowing boat with a billowing sail painted with a great eye. Its oars moved in time to the pulsating chord progression of Vangelis' score for the film *Conquest of Paradise* and the silhouette of a man standing on a raft came into view. Clouds of red smoke filled the air as the rousing music reached a crescendo. Poseidon, god of the ocean, arose from the depths and a great battle ensued, with the man being thrown into the water after his raft caught fire.

It was a story I knew so well. The mythical hero Odysseus lands, naked and exhausted, on the shores of Scheria, the home of the Phaeacians. He surprises the young princess, Nausika, who is taking a break from doing her washing on the shore and is playing ball with her handmaidens. The water's edge is a dangerous place in Greek mythology. It's where young maidens get ravished by gods and demi-gods.

In Homer's tale, Nausika takes Odysseus home to her parents, the gentle King Alkinoos and Queen Arete.

At Paleokastritsa on that August night, Odysseus and the maidens made their way along the shore to the stage, where the hero proceeded to tell the story of the things that had happened to him since leaving Troy ten years before. And then the king gave him a boat so that he could sail to his kingdom of Ithaca, where he would be reunited with his patient wife, Penelope, and his son, who had been waiting for him for twenty years.

The boatmen and divers of Paleokastritsa turned the myth into the most stunning, poignant, surreal, magical and memorable tourist attraction I had ever seen.

But it was not over yet. The music changed to poignant oboe and then the skies lit up with white rockets exploding over the bay.

Even Gorgeous George, who was always hard to impress, had to admit it was pretty special.

'I have not seen anything like it,' he said. And for Gorgeous George, that was high praise indeed.

The humidity was so high, even the Corfiots were complaining. On days and weeks like this I imagined myself to be lounging in some kind of diaphanous dress in shimmering white. I would be a goddess or an ancient princess, waited on hand and foot, too hot and tired and far too important to do anything for myself.

'We are fucked,' said Yanni Pianni. 'We cannot wait until September when the taverna is not so busy. It is just too hot.'

But for holidaymakers on a fortnight's visit, the heat was what they wanted, what they expected. As for us, though, living here all year round, we had found ourselves hiding out of the sun, taking shelter under the vine at the height of its heat.

'You're not as tanned as I thought,' said a friend, fresh in from the UK, and heading straight for a sunbed. It was the last place I wanted to be.

These last few weeks we had been spending at most about ten minutes in the sun after lunch, me to read a book, Andreas to do his sudoku, and then we would head off upstairs for a lie-down. It was the only thing to be done. We finally understood the need for a siesta. It was just too darn hot to do anything else. In conversation with an IT specialist who had come from Athens to Corfu for a job selling entry tickets to a waterpark, he told us he had never experienced heat like it.

'In Athens, in the shade, you are all right,' he says. 'But here, the sweat pours off me even in the shade. It makes me tired and makes my bones ache.'

And when the church bells rang in the heat of an August afternoon, it was even too much for the village dogs. For the first time in months they were silent. Our bundle of hair from next door, now called Aletis, lay panting on Spiros Bear's doorstep.

157

There was great excitement. A new post office was opening up right in the middle of the village on the spot where a menswear shop had operated for a few years back in the long distant past. We had been told it would be open at seven thirty in the morning, so we made our way up to the *plateia*, accompanied by the rising sun and a parcel destined for England.

The post office, however, was closed. If it had been back home, there would have been a ribbon-cutting ceremony, or maybe even a fanfare. But not here. So I had a coffee and a cake in the *plateia* and Andreas went up the steps to pay the water bill. The ladies in the office allowed him to walk out on the balcony like Juan Peron and he took a couple of photos. All was quiet.

And then Thassos arrived from the bakery around the back, his arms full of bread.

We had hit upon the best time of day at this time of year. It was cool before the heat of the sun beat down and made us all turn into sweaty blobs. And then we saw Kostas Elvis, the singing postmaster, having a coffee so we waved to him and he opened up the shop. There was a bit of confusion as he weighed the parcel and worked out the price. He put it on the scales again, just to make sure. It was not only the first parcel to be sent from the new post office, it was the first one heading for England. But we got there in the end. He explained in Greek that he would put the stamps on later, once his son, the real postmaster, had taken the parcel into the bigger post office at Zavros.

A few days later, the parcel had arrived. My friend took a photograph of it. It was covered with nineteen stamps with just a small area revealing the address.

At this time of year, there were festivals going on all over Greece. The festivals might not have been as extravagant as in previous years because of the economic crisis, and some had been cancelled altogether because of the hard times facing the country and its people. But there was one festival that, however bad things were, would be celebrated everywhere. We were in the lead-up to the Orthodox feast day of the Dormition of the Theotokos on 15 August. This was the date on which Christ's mother, the Virgin Mary, died or 'fell asleep' before being taken by her son up into heaven.

It was also a busy time for Saint Spyridon. He was once again taken out of the calm and cool church to be paraded around the town in his casket, accompanied by marching bands and a procession to commemorate his defence of the island against the Turks in 1716.

During these times, we kept our eyes out for signs painted on white sheets at the roadsides to advertise the various *panegyri*. And we relied on posters on telegraph poles to keep abreast of what was going on. Funerals were advertised with just a day's notice. Posters were never taken down; they were just covered by more sheets of A4 proclaiming the latest dead person, church service or local function. It always seemed rather disrespectful for the names of the departed to be covered up by posters advertising a frog festival in Skripero or a blues band playing in a bar in Paleokastritsa.

In the week before Maria Day, as the ex-pats called it, there was a party atmosphere in the *plateia*, with traditional folk music and pagan-like dancing around the church door. Each night there was something different as the anticipation grew.

On the eve of the *panegyri*, the church bells tolled as a procession made its way through the village for a service in the church. In the *plateia*, the men prepared something called *sperna*, soaking great tubs of raisins in water before taking them inside the community hall and locking the doors to mix them up with the boiled wheat, almonds and seeds and maybe a dash of ouzo. And then the key was turned from the inside and the women and children were allowed in to run the production line. Scoops of the mixture were put on a long table, the nimble fingers of the assembly team making quick work of putting it into plastic bags for the service the next day.

As the band struck up the theme music to *Harry Potter*, xylophones gently tinkling, I got up from my seat in the *plateia* to find the best spot to take a photo and some video. The village had become used to me taking photographs of anything that moved and often pointed out things they thought might interest me before I even saw them. It was a magical night, with a throng

159

of people gathered under the trees to listen to the music under a sky of black ink, with a bell tower picked out by spotlight and two lamps illuminating the church door. I half expected the Knight Bus to come roaring through the village, slowing down to inch past the busy tavernas and forcing oncoming traffic to step aside, as coaches did around these parts. Or maybe Hagrid on a motorbike and sidecar.

I clicked off the camera to stop filming and noticed a fluttering beside me. A small bat flapped by. Its wings almost touched the ground. I followed its progress as it wove in and out of the percussion section, swooping low over the timpani and bass drum and then up, higher and higher, to swirl around the bell tower.

To give them credit, the band was so professional that they played on as if this was an entirely usual occurrence, which, quite possibly, it was. And then the band played the theme music to *Lord of the Rings* and 'Gangnam Style' before calling it an evening and heading off for a *souvlaki*.

But you should never leave kettle drums unattended. With the band members safely out of the way, three children seized the drumsticks and had a bit of a bash, an indulgent father smiling and taking photos. Two other children, one each side of the square, pulled out toy whistles from their lucky bags and called to each other like the Scops owls whose voices punctuated the Corfiot summer nights. But the drum roll was enough to disturb two band members during their meal. The teenage boys strode out across the square, young men with stern faces, on a mission to protect their instruments. They snatched back their sticks, had words with the miscreants and then put a cover over the drums before going back to finish their *souvlakia*.

When 15 August arrived, Marias in best clothes and newly-permed hair attended the morning service. There were older men in crisp white shirts and women in blocks of bright colours – orange, yellow, green – and widows in black. There was the usual chanting and some singing; and the congregation made the sign of the cross in formation. Behind the screen of the iconostasis, the priest got to work to make the wine holy. He emerged from the central door with a golden book obscuring

160

his face. The air was thick with incense smoke and the smell of basil as people brushed past the herb, which was potted up in perfect orbs and dotted around the church.

An eighteen-month-old girl was carried in her mother's arms, pigtailed, immaculate, her mother with an elfin crop and halterneck dress with a stiff white collar. The child gazed in wonder at the pretty lights in the chandeliers overhead. Pearls, best earrings and necklaces were all on display. A collection plate was taken around and filled with notes – nobody had much to give away but today, of all days, was special. The money was taken to the back of the church and counted there and then. There was a growler near us, humming deeply along with everything. The doors of the church remained open to let the air in and outside in the *plateia*, a child fell and cried, followed by the sound of village dogs fighting.

A swallow twittered and laughed as the priest gave the children a spoonful of wine and some communion bread. And still the small child gazed at the pretty lights and pointed to them while the *sperna* made last night was brought up the aisle and placed in baskets at the door.

The service over, the bells rang and the *plateia* was buzzing.

In the *kafenio*, Kiki fanned herself with a card and made coffee while her father served a never-ending queue of customers and offered them cake. Some Scandinavian holidaymakers came in looking for dog food to feed a stray.

Spiros Ron's brother, the schoolteacher, smiled, shook my hand and touched my shoulder. Everyone wished each other *xronia polla* – many years. Even Spiros Bear was here today, hair down and newly-washed. Yannis of the Mohican and White Sunglasses arrived on his bike, wearing his customary bell-bottomed jeans and sleeveless T-shirt showing his muscles. He sent Nikos the Dancer from Gardelades to get his tobacco. He still couldn't get off his scooter because the stand was broken; and if he put it on the floor, the engine would flood.

The rich, onion and meat aroma of a bubbling *stifado* spilled out from the tavernas. They would be busy tonight for the *panegyri*.

And then the priest came out of the church in his long black robe and headed for home.

It was early evening but still not a table to be found in the *plateia*. Each one was reserved with a name scrawled on a piece of cardboard and secured with pieces of marble slab.

'It's ridiculous,' one ex-pat said. 'We can't find anywhere to sit.'

So we thought about our base for the evening – and we knew we would need a base with all that eating, drinking and dancing, especially in this heat. It was only the two of us but things weren't looking too promising.

'You can sit with us!' Betty's husband, Antonis, shouted over, throwing a bag of lamb on to a table. 'You are part of our family now.'

Betty was slaving over a hot stove in Spirodoula's, as she had been all summer. No dancing in the *plateia* for her tonight. Instead, the children were out with their father and we were soon joined by Koula and Ilias and assorted members of the family. For a short while, it included Spiros Bear and Natalia. But dancing was not in the Bear's repertoire, even though it was in his genes. The day we saw Spiros dancing would be the day Hades froze over.

There were beers, soft drinks, balloon sellers and doughnuts, *xronia polla* said at every turn, dancing around the trees and children tearing around everywhere.

Ilias gestured to me and made a shape with his hands to indicate that he wanted me to take a picture.

'Photo, Margarita,' he said, gesturing to the church.

I followed him and Koula where they posed next to the rail in front of the iconostasis, which was full of basil plants they had grown especially for the occasion. Back in the *plateia*, Spiros Ron's brother, the schoolteacher with a charming smile, led the line of dancers, a red handkerchief linking him to his sprightly wife. She tipped her head to us as she passed by.

Nikos from Gardelades spun around and around on his own, like a top, changing T-shirts every now and then and cooling himself off with water from the village pump. During the course of the evening, I counted at least seven tops pulled from his rucksack. He was like a conjuror performing a magic trick. There was a Barcelona T-shirt, one bearing the face of Che Guevara, a

162

white one, a Communist Party one, a blue and white football shirt with Maradona emblazoned across the back, a green one for Panathinaikos FC, and a light blue one bearing the words 'Brooklyn Circus'.

Nikos danced his own dance, unfettered and totally unconnected to anyone in the long line around him. The basic Greek dance, I had come to learn, was relatively easy. You joined hands with the people next to you and just followed the one on your right, following the beat and putting a little skip in between. I am sure there are more complicated steps than that but it seemed to work and no-one laughed at how bad I was. Then the tempo changed, the dance became faster and it went on, and on, and on. My hands slipped through the fingers of others, and sweat poured off my neck, breastbone, temples and back as I went round and round the trees in this repetitive workout, which was strenuous but fun. The best thing was never to look down at your feet, but to just follow the beat and your heart.

Back at the table, I was about to go back home to use the lavatory. I had come to realise that to use the *kafenio* toilet at the side of the building, you had to be either very drunk or desperate.

'Where you going, Margarita?' someone said. When I told them, I was swiftly raised from my chair and pointed in the direction of the community hall.

'But...'

'No, you go there, it's much better.'

The hall was full of wild children, hiding behind curtains and riding on sack trucks. I sat inside the WC, my foot against the door as there was no lock.

Out in the *plateia*, big Nikos the President was doing a pigeon dance, with Lovejoy and his brother crouching on their haunches beside him and slow clapping. For a big man, Nikos was surprisingly graceful. And then Andreas, fresh from selling raffle tickets, appeared and did the pigeon dance with him.

'He is at home here, no?' Antonis said from our table.

He was indeed. The thing about Andreas is that he can fit in anywhere. It had taken me a little longer. But now, our Greek village felt completely like home.

We left just after three in the morning and still they were dancing the night away.

The party was over. That was it for another year.

It was quiet now after all our village festivities.

A cool wind whipped through the *plateia* as a handful of people sat under the Narnia lamp post. And it was bliss.

A week after the *panegyri*, and still the days and nights were humid. There was a pair of solitary workboots which had been standing on a village building site for the last few days. I was rather concerned that their owner had vaporised.

'The weather will start to change after the 15th,' we were told by our weatherman Canadian George, as the summer celebrations built up to their crescendo.

With the end of our long line of visiting family and friends, things had become calmer but the weather was still hot. After almost ten months in Greece, I was no longer like a holidaymaker, craving for sun. I sat in the shade whenever I could. I enjoyed the early mornings, when the days were at their coolest. How chambermaids coped with changing hotel beds and cleaning in this heat was beyond me. They deserved a medal rather than a pittance. And I now understood why a siesta was so important to the people who worked in this heat all day. It ground you down, it wore you out.

But as the sweat poured in rivulets down my back one night, something rather marvellous happened. We knew it was coming because had had a phone call from Corfu Town from Spiros Bear. He wanted us to remove the tools from the back of his truck and put them under cover.

'It's pouring with rain here,' he said. 'It will reach you soon.'

And, sure enough, twenty minutes later, the thunder and lightning began, bouncing off the mountains that surrounded our village stage like the seating in an amphitheatre. It was the first rain we'd had since Easter. It lasted at most about half an hour. But enough time to dance in it in the dark.

'Shall we?' Andreas said.

And he led me from the terrace down the steps to the parched lawn under the palm tree.

'Cha-cha-cha or waltz?' he said. He'd always been very proud of his cha-cha-cha.

'Waltz, I think.'

So we danced in the dark in the rain. I think Zeus and Co were up in the gods of the amphitheatre looking down. But I didn't care. I danced for all I was worth.

A ropey old ambulance was parked in the square. The Perspex around the blue light was broken and the livery was peeling off. The door to the village hall was open and men laughed as they walked in and out. Something was going on inside but there was a certain casualness to it all, a frivolity I couldn't quite work out.

'What's happening?' I asked Kiki. And then the penny dropped when I saw sticking plasters on people's arms.

'They are giving blood,' she said.

Nikos the president arrived on his big Harley-style motorcycle, mirrored shades on, looking every inch the easy rider. He strolled into the hall and took his place with the rest.

With less than two months before our Big Fat Greek Gap Year came to an end, we began to think about all the packing up that needed to be done and the journey home. We also thought about ways we could make these twelve months away turn into another year, but without the homesickness. Ideally, I would have liked the best of both worlds: the ability to live in two different but equally lovely villages. A foot in Corfu and a foot in in Dorset. But it was a long stretch, and I'd never been able to do the splits. Our Corfu village had everything. Beauty, friendly people, warmth in heat and warmth in spirit. And we'd seen it through autumn, winter, spring and now summer. What an experience. It had been incredible.

You couldn't have had a better and more conveniently situated village on the whole of the island. Twenty-five minutes on a good road into town and five minutes by car to the sea. Three good tavernas which were open all year round and the most excellent mini-market and *kafenio* where you could sit and watch the world go by. A filling station down the road, a butcher's, and the most wonderful landscape right on our doorstep.

And now we had tamed the overgrown Sleeping Beauty garden and painted inside the house it was better than perfect. I had read around sixty books, including some very fat ones indeed, which was good for someone with the attention span of a goldfish.

On the beach at San Stefanos – the one on Corfu's north west tip, rather than the posh one on the other side – the wind was howling, umbrellas were flapping wildly and the breakers rushed up to meet the shore.

We walked along the long stretch of sand to a point where the sunbeds ran out. A naked man and his topless wife sat in front of a small tent and an exposed, flat shelf of rock.

The tattoo on his arm could have said *gatekeeper*.

I kept my head down and just followed in my husband's footsteps.

A little farther along, a young man and woman painted each other with sloppy sand. It was as if they were in a commercial for *Sure* deodorant or something. There were a few stray souls who had on swimsuits but as we rounded the corner, we were confronted by more naked bodies. I don't know about you, and I'm not sure what Jesus would have done in this situation, but I couldn't help but *look*.

A man crouched behind a bush to put his shorts back on. I turned away and my eye was almost taken out by a flapping appendage attached to another man just walking past. A woman a little farther along bent over, on purpose, I am sure. Andreas did not know where to look. So we stared up at the cliffs above our heads. An interesting formation against a clear blue sky. And then a large man with nothing on walked out of the sea with his wife who was in just bikini bottoms. He could have been wearing a thong but if he was, it had been eaten by his large buttocks. If ever there was a case for someone wearing a burka, this man would have been it.

At the end of the beach, the sand and the people ran out. We had no towels – we had come totally unprepared for a swim as we had just fancied a walk. Andreas stripped off and gambolled into the waves like a puppy unleashed. And I stood on the shore holding my Birkenstocks and his flip-flops, like a forlorn

Paddington Bear waiting in the waves. I looked out to sea like Meryl Streep in The French Lieutenant's Woman. Andreas was having such *fun*.

The sea roared and crashed onto the sand and he dived in and out of the surf like a dolphin. A large one, it was true, but graceful nonetheless.

It was tempting.

There was nobody there to see, and if there were, who cared? My body was better than Burka Man's any day. So I took my clothes off daintily, folded them up on the beach and ran right in. It was exhilarating as the waves crashed over my head and salt water filled my mouth. It was a wonderful feeling.

Enjoy the moment. If nothing else, my big fat grown-up Greek gap year had taught me that.

Part V

Autumn

There was an Old Man of Corfu
Who never knew what he should do
So he rushed up and down, till the sun made him brown
That bewildered Old Man of Corfu.

Edward Lear

September, October and November

The smell of pine wafted down through the hillside as we wallowed in the warm sea at our favourite beach, Yialaskari. We picked our way out of the water over the pebbles, dried ourselves and then strolled up to the only taverna in this isolated little spot to settle down for freshly grilled fish and giant prawns. The smell of garlic and freshly-applied suntan lotion wafted through the air. The days were still baking hot. Skin could still burn.

It was strange to think we would be leaving all this behind.

The nights were beginning to get cooler. It didn't stop the dogs barking, their voices reverberating around our village and the valley, night and day, day and night. It was a sound I had become used to but one I wouldn't miss. In a few weeks, we would be heading for home on the ferry to Ancona before driving across northern Italy and into France and then sailing across the channel.

A strong wind blew through the trees in the *plateia*. It whooshed and roared as it wound its way through the leaves. Autumn was around the corner. And then, just as suddenly, the wind subsided. As Michalis brought us out our coffee, he stopped to speak to four old men, including Theodoros, sitting outside the *kafenio*.

'You *have* to stay in this village,' he said, walking over to us. 'You will live to long age.'

He pointed to the old men.

'They are ninety-one, ninety-three, eighty-seven and eighty-three.'

The old men beamed, to emphasise the point.

'Why do people live so long here?' I asked.

Michalis placed the cups on our table.

He looked around him. I thought he was going to say something about the blue sky, a simple life, the Mediterranean diet.

He took a deep breath as he revealed their secret.

'It is very simple,' he said. 'They talk, talk, talk. It is like Duracell battery, they don't stop.'

Human interaction and friendship. It made the big world a smaller place.

Michalis picked up the tray and waved to a hire car which was attempting to drive past the *kafenio* towards the dead end. It had happened all through the tourist season. And then a van went by Elizabeth's, selling clothing and cheap shoes, the driver jibber-jabbering about his wares. The van stopped and the driver got into a conversation with a woman who peered in through his window. Their voices were like rapid gunfire, topped off by the woman saying *oxi, oxi,* and all through the loudspeaker, which the driver had forgotten to turn off.

There was a burst of activity as the swallows prepared to leave the *plateia* and head back to warmer climes. The nests had long been empty and it was time for the parents and the children to go. I counted seventeen of them sitting in a long line on the telephone wire, flexing their wings and comparing notes in preparation for the journey ahead. I looked around and noticed a single wellington boot on the fountain. Autumn was almost here, although one welly did not make a winter.

It was the end of the season. During the day, a few open-mouthed holidaymakers strolled around at a snail's pace. There were now grapes on sale at the roadside, instead of watermelons in the summer and potatoes in winter. The tavernas wound down, many of them about to either close completely or operate only at weekends. Aeroplanes still flew overhead but the flights were not as frequent. And down in the olive groves, the grass under the trees was cut and ready for the nets to be placed underneath. It would not be long before harvest.

In the evenings in the *plateia*, the card players sat at the tables outside the *kafenio* in the gloom, yelling at the hands they'd been dealt and the moves their opponents were making. Then, at eight o'clock, the lights in the Narnia lamp post came on as if by magic, along with the two lamps outside the church door, to illuminate the scene. The children roared around on bicycles and played tag, using the war memorial as 'home'.

In the *kafenio* there was fierce nodding when it was announced on the television that the far right party, Golden Dawn, appeared to have finally had its come-uppance. Its leaders had been arrested for crimes against democracy while the world looked on.

'A prostitute is worth a hundred politics,' said an old man. 'At least she is honest.'

The grapes on our vine were fat, black and ready for picking. But we didn't have time to harvest our crop so bequeathed them to Koula so that she could make her famous family wine.

We drove to Corfu Airport, our last pick-up of the year, to welcome my brother-in-law and his wife. They were grabbing two weeks while they still could.

Back at the Villa Oleander, the four of us rubbed down the grilles outside in preparation for painting them, something we should have done earlier in the year but had not because we'd been packed to the rafters with visitors. We spent two days in our painting gear before moving on to the garden with pruning shears and clippers to shape the oleander before it had a chance to bolt again next year. It was sad doing all of this, because we wouldn't be here to appreciate it. But we felt it was good for the house to be put to bed properly and given a little bit of tender loving care before the next occupants moved in.

We were having an ouzo in the *plateia* as the card players yelled around us when Andreas made a pronouncement.

'Of course,' he said. 'We don't have to leave, you know.'

Leave? In the early months of our Greek gap year, there was nothing I had wanted to do more. I needed to go home, I had to go home. Every part of my body ached for home. Yet there was something about this place that had worked its magic. I couldn't imagine not being connected to it any more. But I also knew I needed to be in Dorset. And I wasn't sure there was a way of having both.

My brother-in-law cleared his throat.

'Well, we've been thinking,' he said, looking at his wife.

'Yes?' I said, wondering what was coming next.

173

'Well, we were wondering whether maybe we could rent it together?'

And it was as simple as that. Another year at the Villa Oleander but with more time back in England. The perfect solution.

The next morning and word had already got out. The doorbell rang and Ilias was standing there, smoking a cigarette and proffering a large, blue plastic bag containing two huge slabs of pork – enough for eight casseroles – ten big, fat pork chops and twelve thick slices of belly pork, all lean, meaty and with no smell. These were the pigs our kitchen scraps, put in a bag and left on the gate every couple of days for collection, had been feeding on.

'I think we're meant to put it into the freezer, for the months ahead,' my husband said.

'There's enough meat there for the whole winter,' I answered.

'I think that's the idea.'

And then my sister-in-law took one look at the contents of the bag and shuddered.

'Ugh, pork,' she said. 'I don't like the fact that you've been feeding these pigs and now we're going to be eating them.'

Better a pig that's been loved and known rather than one that ends up as an anonymous slice of white meat shrink-wrapped in a supermarket refrigerator. But each to their own.

As we unpacked the meat and put it into bags labelled *Village Pork*, there was another ring at the doorbell. There stood Spiros Bear, leaning against the porch and smoking a cigarette.

'You come to my house tonight,' he said. 'We have pork in oven.'

Luckily, my sister-in-law was upstairs so did not hear what we were going to have for supper. Imagine, though, the look of horror on her face – and, I have to admit, also on mine – when we arrived at Spiros' house later that evening. He opened the door of his outside pizza oven and Aletis the little dog barked with joy. He got hold of a large paddle to pull out a tray containing a huge foil parcel. He unwrapped it and the steam escaped. The clouds parted to reveal a perfect pig's head, blind-eyed but grinning like a dinosaur.

174

He took a long-bladed knife and sliced through the head, like a spoon through jelly.

'It is…what you say? It is delicacy.'

I took his word for it and had a tiny bit of cheek to show willing but chose to pass on the brain. Luckily, there was not enough of that to go around. For so-called smart animals, pigs had surprisingly small brains, especially when their heads were cooked. Luckily, Spiros was aware that we English could be rather squeamish and had prepared some pork loin along with roast potatoes and salad. My sister-in-law and I had extra helpings of salad to bulk up the plate so we didn't feel obliged to eat a snout or tongue or something worse.

'We have some good news,' Andreas said, raising a glass of Ribena. 'We're renting the house for another year.'

'I knew you stay,' Spiros said. 'They tell me at *kafenio*.'

He passed us two crispy ears as a reward for our good sense.

'What's that you have there?' said Canadian George, pulling up a chair in the *plateia*.

I handed him a long card Betty had given us that morning when we had taken up the latest bag of vegetable peelings for the pigs.

'It's Yorgi and Eleni's wedding,' he said, reading it. 'Are you going to go?'

There was no question about it. Of course we were. A big fat Greek wedding to end our twelve months here? It couldn't have been better.

'That's good,' he said. 'We've been invited too.'

We had been in this village for a year and it was only now that we discovered Canadian George, who was one of our favourite people, was related to 'our' family. So many people in this village were related to one another, it was an honour for us to have been invited. We felt very excited to be a part of it.

The wedding was to take place in the bride's village of Potamos, near Corfu Town, and would be followed by a reception at a local hotel. The service didn't start until five o'clock because of the heat.

'You'll love it,' Canadian George said. 'There'll be plenty of dancing.'

A few days before the wedding, I drove Betty into town to look for a new dress. As the bridegroom's sister-in-law and mother of the bridesmaid, it was important she looked good. I had already decided I would make do with a trusty little black dress. I didn't have the money to get anything new. Betty tried on a few dresses in the Hondos Centre, Corfu's only department store, and was like a child in a sweet shop.

'I haven't bought any clothes since I was having Marie Angela,' she confided, as she gazed in the mirror at an elegant woman in a long dress looking back at her.

She tried on another and liked it very much. I didn't, but wasn't sure how to tell her. Luckily, Spiros Bear's daughter Marianna arrived, having just finished her shift at one of the bars on the Liston. She urged Betty to visit another shop before making a decision.

'It did not look good on her,' she whispered to me.

In a small boutique a few streets away from the Hondos Centre, Betty emerged from the changing room, a vision in dark green, a beautiful colour which matched her eyes. She looked stunning, the fifties-style dress flattering her slim figure and clinging to her hips as it fell to the ground. Her radiance as she looked in the mirror was breathtaking, a surprised smile fixed on her face. Even she could see how lovely she looked. And then the assistant handed her a gold bolero which she put over her bare shoulders. Stunning. With her hair up, Betty was an Eastern European princess. She looked absolutely gorgeous.

Sitting outside a bar after our successful morning's shop, I decided I wanted to have at least something new for the wedding. So I went into a shoe shop across the way and came out with a pair of red and leopard print shoes with peep toes and four-inch heels. They were totally impractical, of course. So just about perfect.

Two days before the wedding and we were squeezed into the bedroom of Yorgi and Eleni's new house next to Lambis's in the olive groves. The house Yorgi had built with his uncle was full of candles, friends and lots of sweets. Young unmarried women and girls were preparing the bed, making a big flourish of putting on the sheet and smoothing it down before loading up the pillowcases. Taking hold of the corners, they threw out the counterpane, which was a tricky manoeuvre because the room was full of chattering people. The crowd overflowed onto the balcony.

There were gunshots outside and *panegyri* music playing at full blast on the stereo in the living room. And then handfuls of rice, rose petals and money were tossed onto the bed along with assorted young members of the family. A bewildered Marie Angela, recovering from a cold, was thrown on first, closely followed by a young, female cousin and then a brother or two. The bed's strength was then tested to the hilt as Ilias, the bridegroom's father and as big as a bear, jumped on the mattress to a huge roar of laughter, punctuated by the sound of rice being crunched underfoot as relatives drew closer to get a good photo. They would be finding rice in the bed for weeks to come.

'You take photo, Margarita,' Ilias said to me, gesturing for the crowds to allow me safe passage to get closer to the action. And then the family lined up for pictures, with the main focus on the dishevelled bed. The bed-making ritual was a big tradition in the lead-up to the wedding. It was meant to bring the newly-wed couple luck in the bedroom department.

Outside, my husband lined up with Yorgi and the bridegroom's brothers, Antonis and Simos, to fire their guns in the air. They laughed at Spiros Bear, who was wielding his gun like a pump-action Rambo.

'I no like guns,' he said. A stone-faced Natalia stood by his side, in a smart shirt, cigarette pants and heels as high as Mount Pantokrator. She cradled a shotgun as if it were a baby and the weapon looked rather too comfortable in her arms. She aimed, she shot – she was a natural. I made a mental note to myself never to get the wrong side of Natalia.

And then the *panegyri* music began again and was turned up to its loudest, the bride's mother bringing out a speaker and putting it on the windowsill. The happy couple emerged from the front porch to lead a Greek dance around the lawn, looks of pure joy on the bride's face and nervous tension on the groom's.

And there, in the sky, was a new moon.

'What's the name for that in Greek?' I asked Canadian George's wife, Sophia, as I pointed to the sky from the balcony. It was the first time we had met and I liked her immediately, even though neither of us spoke much of the other's language. That evening we had been communicating by gestures and had rubbed each other's shoulders and said *bravo* every time we made the other understand.

'*Fengari*,' Sophia said in her breathy accent. She could have been the love child of Melina Mercouri and Sophia Loren if that had been possible. At that moment, rather obligingly, someone put 'Never on a Sunday' on the stereo.

'*Fengari*? That's beautiful,' I said.

'And in English?' Sophia said, patting my back.

'Moon.'

'Ah, *muhn*.' Even the way she said it in English was beautiful.

During our year away, we had been determined to get fitter and lose weight. We had walked regularly around the olive groves, eaten more sensibly and exercised to a video three times a week. Much of this, however, fell to pieces during the summer when we had visitors to stay. The day before the wedding was weigh day. At 100 kilos, Andreas was heavier than he had been when he came here. At 68 kilos, I was only a kilo lighter. But we didn't care. We laughed as we squeezed ourselves into our wedding outfits to make sure they were all right for the following day. I told him to go downstairs so I could put my hair up and manoeuvre my feet into my new shoes. I found a leopard print scarf I had brought with me from England and tied it around my neck. I was ready to make the tricky journey down the steps.

'You can open your eyes now,' I said, when I had reached the bottom.

Andreas whistled.

'Wow, you look stunning.'

'Thank you,' I said. 'You don't look so bad yourself.'

It had been some time since I had seen him in a suit. It made such a change from painting trousers and baggy shorts.

He took my hand and we did a slow waltz around the room.

'I think it's going to be fun tomorrow, don't you?' he said.

I thought so too. But I'd have to hunt out some flat shoes to put in my handbag. There was no way I was going to be able to walk very far in these skyscrapers, let alone dance.

It was the morning of the wedding and we were sitting under the vine having our breakfast.

'I don't think I've ever seen so much blue,' Andreas said, gazing at the sky.

There was a faint ringing sound, like Tinkerbell, and it grew louder as what it was attached to drew closer. Aletis shot in, round as a barrel now and as excited as ever to see us.

Andreas scooped him up, pushing the map of Italy and France that was on the table to one side. We had been route planning for the journey home and hoped it wouldn't be quite as eventful as the drive down.

'So what has this year done for you?' he said, tickling the little dog under the chin but talking to me. 'Have you changed in any way? Have you found yourself?'

It sounded a little profound and rather unlike us really. I stopped to think about it. I knew this year away had given him the peace and tranquillity he needed to lower his blood pressure. Andreas had mellowed over the last twelve months. But what had it done for me? I'd become more tolerant, for sure, and realised it was true that you never knew what you had until you didn't have it. The overpowering feeling of homesickness, for my Dorset landscape, my family, friends and village life had been with me from the outset and it had accompanied me throughout the year, like a wound taking its time to heal. But I had come to terms with it and no longer felt guilty for feeling that way. I had missed my independence in monetary terms but, by sticking to routine and then embracing an equal amount of spontaneity, what I had rediscovered and nourished was my creative side, which had been pestering me for more years than I cared to remember.

It had been a good year.

On the road outside our house, the vehicles began to assemble. Antonis jumped out of the driver's seat, with Betty and the children waving inside the car, and walked down the drive to fix a red scarf to our wing mirror.

'You must come now,' he said. 'It is time.'

A large hire car with Simos at the wheel and carrying his brother, the bridegroom, and their mother and father, Koula and Ilias, was parked in front of the bins while the fat cats looked on. As all the cars backed up behind us, the bridegroom's party pulled away to lead the convoy down the hill, tooting their horns at passing traffic and picking up other cars along the way. Red scarves flew in the autumn air, set against a sky of bright blue. Lambis's car joined us as we reached the bottom of his lane and then we drove into town, horns tooting all the way to the hospital and then on towards Potamos. Just before we got into the village, we parked in front of a factory building belonging to the bride's father.

'We walk from here,' Antonis said.

I looked down at my shoes.

'The church is not far,' he said.

Betty made a face as if to say *'oh yes it is'* but there was nothing to be done other than go for it. With her high wedges under her flowing gown, she and I shuffled along the uneven tarmac to the bride's house, along with little Marie Angela, not yet four, whose white, hooped bridesmaid's dress swayed as she walked. *Mummy's little princess* is a phrase you hear a lot these days, its overuse filling little girls with a narcissism and hubris they simply don't need. But that day it's true to say that Marie Angela really did look as if she'd stepped out from the pages of a fairy tale.

The bride's house was in the middle of Potamos and there was a party on the terrace. With the male members of his family, the groom went on to the church to wait for his bride at the door. A crowd of villagers lingered outside the bride's front gate and, to the sound of gunfire, accordion, guitar, song and applause, the bride emerged in a long, simple white gown, with straps, a decorated bodice and a flattering fitted skirt, so unlike some of the meringue dresses I had seen in the pictures outside the photographers' studios in Corfu Town. Eleni walked arm-in-arm with her father, with Mariangela tagging on behind.

The band led the parade, playing the traditional song 'Simera Gamos Ginete', which translates to 'there's a wedding today'.

Betty and I followed with the other guests through the village's main street to the church steps, which were decorated with flowers and green and white lanterns. At the door, the bride and groom were reunited to more applause before walking into the church. Inside, there were four priests, including our own. The service took a lifetime under the hot lights of the ornate chandeliers. Every now and then people dived outside for a cigarette or a break from the heat, although it was unseasonably warm in the streets and even my nail polish began to melt.

The female guests looked like models in a magazine, overly made-up and glowing with foundation and blusher, tight hairstyles and shoes even higher than mine. Spiros Bear was almost as smart as he had been at Easter when he carried the banner to the church. Beside him, Natalia was a striking picture of Russian confidence and sophistication, in a short black dress and high heels. And then the bells began to ring, a two-tone song rather than an English peal, signalling that the service was over. So we all headed back into the church where the bride and groom and their families stood in a horseshoe shape at the altar, ready to receive guests who crunched their way through the rice that had been thrown all over the floor. As we waited our turn, Canadian George ducked when Little Ilias and Marie Angela declared a rice-fight war. There was rice everywhere.

'Don't worry,' Canadian George said, seeing the look on my face. 'They pay for cleaners.'

So I knelt down as best I could in those blessed shoes and picked up a handful of rice from the floor and threw it rather nonchalantly at Little Ilias. As usual, my aim was pretty poor and I ended up showering our priest on the shoulder.

He turned around and glared at me. But only for a moment. Then he smiled. He should do that more often, I thought. It lit up his face.

After the bride and groom had headed off for the reception, I struggled in my heels as I made my way back to our car with my husband and Antonis. The groom's hire car swished and then stopped.

'Yassoo, Margarita-mou,' Koula said, unleashing an avalanche of Greek I didn't understand. I was never going to learn this language.

'They tell you to get in the car,' Antonis said. 'You cannot walk with those on your feet.'

By the time we reached the Luna d'Argenta, one of the island's most popular venues for wedding receptions, it was dark. Under the cover of the night, I eased out of my shoes and slipped into something more comfortable. Inside, we found our table and the lights were lowered as the bride and groom walked in to 'Simera Gamos Ginete', the guests standing up and clapping and the bride's train flowing out behind her. They walked onto the dance floor in front of a wedding cake which had been placed on a stand that looked like an upturned sousaphone, a nod to the island's philharmonic band heritage. And then the onslaught began, with copious amounts of Greek dancing and smoking in between courses of food and a never-ending supply of wine for us and Coke for Spiros Bear. There was cheese, cured meats, salad, taramasalata and tzatziki and dancing. Mixed plate of aubergine, cheese pie, chips, roasted stuffed pepper, meat ball, village sausage and dancing. Cheesecake and dancing. Baclava and dancing. Coffee and dancing. And wine, lots of wine. And dancing. It really was a wonder no-one was sick. There was a table full of smiling priests, a photographer capturing vignettes around the room and, on the dance floor, my husband doing his now infamous pigeon mating ritual with the village president and assorted moustachioed men.

'You very good,' Natalia said to him, rather too enthusiastically for my liking, as he returned to our table. And then the band played a medley of pop songs and, up near the stage, a little bit of dirty dancing got underway, with the president and his lady friend leading the charge. I got up from the table and tilted my head at my husband.

'You dancing?'

'You asking?'

'I'm dancing.'

He took my hand and we glided across the dance floor, doing our best Patrick Swayze and Baby impersonation to whoops and hollers from the sidelines. Without building myself up too much, I think it's fair to say we stormed the dance floor. People moved to the sidelines when the band began to play 'Dancing Queen'. They cheered and sang along to the chorus.

'You are a very good dancer,' said my new best friend Sophia when we had finished.

'Thank you,' I said. 'I love to dance.'

'You dance very well,' said another man with a moustache who then turned to Andreas and shook him by the hand. 'You are the best.'

And my husband turned to me, kissed my hand and said: '*We* are the best. We are okay.'

And it's true, we were. Opposites attract. We were chalk and cheese, Dionysus and Hestia.

At 7.30 in the morning, the church bells clanged to the accompaniment of a thousand howling dogs. The sun struggled to make it up over the mountain, beaten back by the downpour during the night. Down in the valley the guns popped and, under our window, the geese laughed at having once again kept us awake with their dirty jokes. The crowing cockerels were joined by a new one which couldn't quite reach the last doodle *doo*. A beaten-up old scooter chugged by, in tandem with the gunfire.

It was our final day in the village and the last swallows had, like us, packed up house and were about to begin the long journey home.

Our bags and boxes ready, we headed up into the *plateia* one last time, at least for this year.

The sun beat down. It was still baking hot and, next door, our Spiros Bear, strong as an ox and true to form, was chopping up a great pile of wood. He wore just shorts, a bandana and work boots and bellowed instructions at Natalia to keep her stacking straight. She bellowed back in Russian, giving as good as she got.

On the roadside, Kostas Lovejoy loaded roof tiles into his truck. He stopped to shake our hands and wish us good luck.

'When you come back?' he said.

'December,' we said in unison. There was no way we were going to miss Spiros Bear's name day party, even though we hadn't yet been invited.

We walked up into the village and sat outside Elizabeth's, where a year earlier we had watched dogs mating. A stray dog came along and lay at our feet while we ate our village sausage, moussaka and Greek salad. Nikos, the village president, gave us a toot as he came home from work in his big, smart Mercedes. Spiros Runner shuffled past in bright green trainers and Antonis and his team of painters and decorators arrived to unload their gear. Antonis sauntered over and handed us a small bottle.

'It is for you,' he said. 'For the journey home.'

Home-made *tsipouro*.

'We will see you again, I think. I go off now for sleep.'

The purple bus, *Michaelis 1*, disgorged the schoolchildren and then a van driver parked his vehicle in the *plateia* and hung out winter coats for passers-by to haggle over. George-He-Have-Big-Tractor plopped by on a new scooter; and Canadian George stopped for a chat with a bag of mandarins scrumped from Ilias's land while the latter dug a grave. The Albanian handyman, Kosta, gave us a salute as he, like a modern-day Old Father Time, strolled by with his strimmer over his shoulder Outside the *kafenio*, Kiki cleared a table and squeezed dear Theodoros on the shoulder and she gave us a wave.

This was our village. These were our friends.

The bug-eyed cat, safe for another winter thanks to the efforts of an Englishwoman, promenaded past, just in front of an English couple from an animal rescue charity who were walking with purpose, on the lookout for cats to neuter. And then the church bell tolled mournfully as an old, gold Volvo estate car, carrying a coffin in the back, headed for the *plateia*.

We left the village with the words of Spiros Bear ringing in our ears.

'You ring me when you come back. I will pick you up from airport.'

We were leaving today but we would return.

It was a good feeling.

We leant on the deck rail of the ferry boat *Agios Irini* as she headed towards the mainland where we would pick up a boat to Ancona. In the distance, the sun went down slowly in the mountains above our village. There was a pink, magical glow over the rooftops of Corfu Town as the fading, glorious light hit the spire of St Spyridon's Church. The waterfront gems of the capital's architecture glistened as the ferry made its way past the old fort and the boats bobbing around it. The distinctive silhouette of the island flashed up and then was gone with the coming of the night. It was the mirror image of when we had arrived at sunrise twelve months before.

We held hands as we breathed in the clean air and then stepped aside for a party of black-robed priests, with pony tails, beards and serene smiles. I smiled back. Priests no longer rattled me. We turned to go inside and headed for the bar.

'Hold on a minute,' Andreas said, bringing out a hip flask from his pocket. 'Let's make a toast.'

So we rummaged around in my rucksack for two plastic cups and raised our *tsipouro* as the old town of Corfu disappeared into the dusk.

'To Andreas and Margarita,' he said.

And we downed our *tsipouro* in one.

Epilogue

I am swimming in the sea in a sheltered cove on Corfu's west coast, the warm water rippling through my fingers. I hear the Odysseus tripper boat in the distance and then all is quiet again as it heads back to Paleokastritsa. I swim to the shallows and pick my way out across the shingle, grab a towel from my sunbed on the beach and climb the ramp to the solitary taverna where Andreas is sitting at a table with a grilled sea bream to share and a small jug of crisp white wine ready to pour.

And then the warm, clear air evaporates and I wake up from my daydream. I'm gazing into the flames of an open fire in the front room of our house in Dorset, with my Odysseus, my Dionysus, by my side watching the football on television. And through the over-excited commentary I can hear the village church bells ringing for evensong. The six bells ring quickly, melodically, one after the other, their peal changing into the tune of *Whittington*, which the future Lord Mayor of London was said to have heard when he was leaving the city: *Turn again Whit-ting-ton, turn again Whit-ting-ton*. The bells' sound, as it travels across the village square and down the chimney, is so English and so tuneful. And then I drift off again, peering into those flames and hearing the clanging of our village bells in Corfu. I can see the glowing coals under the lamb as it rotates on the spit. I can smell of its juices and see the smoke wafting across the *plateia* in the evening light. There is Kiki and her family, diligently picking up glasses to take back inside the *kafenio* and the smiling faces of dozens, scores and hundreds of people, with hands joined, dancing in a circle around the trees. Their teeth dazzle from the lights strung out overhead. The sweet smell of basil drifts out from the church. I picture myself, sitting at a table with friends, English and Greek, savouring the salty and garlicky taste of oily roast potatoes, washed down by a glass of President Nikos' wine. And then, from nowhere, two soft hands place themselves

186

in mine. In my head and in the flames, I see the clear smile of Betty and the pretty eyes of Canadian George's wife, Sophia, gently pulling me to join the dance as Andreas, Koula, Lambis, Ilias, Antonis, little Ilias and Marie Angela and even our own Spiros Bear and Natalia move joyously to the music. The circle gets bigger as more and more friends and family attach themselves to the line. I say a quick prayer to Hestia, my goddess of choice these days, shut my eyes tightly and relive the dream.

Lightning Source UK Ltd.
Milton Keynes UK
UKOW01f0021081016

284703UK00003B/62/P